THIS IS YOUR **PASSBOOK**® FOR ...

BRICKLAYER

NLC®

NATIONAL LEARNING CORPORATION®
passbooks.com

PASSBOOK® SERIES

THE *PASSBOOK® SERIES* has been created to prepare applicants and candidates for the ultimate academic battlefield – the examination room.

At some time in our lives, each and every one of us may be required to take an examination – for validation, matriculation, admission, qualification, registration, certification, or licensure.

Based on the assumption that every applicant or candidate has met the basic formal educational standards, has taken the required number of courses, and read the necessary texts, the *PASSBOOK® SERIES* furnishes the one special preparation which may assure passing with confidence, instead of failing with insecurity. Examination questions – together with answers – are furnished as the basic vehicle for study so that the mysteries of the examination and its compounding difficulties may be eliminated or diminished by a sure method.

This book is meant to help you pass your examination provided that you qualify and are serious in your objective.

The entire field is reviewed through the huge store of content information which is succinctly presented through a provocative and challenging approach – the question-and-answer method.

A climate of success is established by furnishing the correct answers at the end of each test.

You soon learn to recognize types of questions, forms of questions, and patterns of questioning. You may even begin to anticipate expected outcomes.

You perceive that many questions are repeated or adapted so that you can gain acute insights, which may enable you to score many sure points.

You learn how to confront new questions, or types of questions, and to attack them confidently and work out the correct answers.

You note objectives and emphases, and recognize pitfalls and dangers, so that you may make positive educational adjustments.

Moreover, you are kept fully informed in relation to new concepts, methods, practices, and directions in the field.

You discover that you arre actually taking the examination all the time: you are preparing for the examination by "taking" an examination, not by reading extraneous and/or supererogatory textbooks.

In short, this PASSBOOK®, used directedly, should be an important factor in helping you to pass your test.

BRICKLAYER

DUTIES AND RESPONSIBILITIES
Under direction, lays brick and masonry to line and grade in or on a given structure or form of work; performs related work.

EXAMPLES OF TYPICAL TASKS
Lays brick or masonry or units in the particular bond specified for walls and partitions. Works with refractory and insulating units for boiler settings and combustion chambers. Does fireproofing, block arching, terra cotta cutting and setting. Constructs brick masonry sewers and manholes. Estimates materials required for small jobs. Keeps job and other records. Reads and follows plans and specifications. May supervise assigned personnel.

SCOPE OF THE EXAMINATION
The written test will be of multiple-choice type and may contain questions designed to test for: knowledge of basic masonry materials, construction, maintenance and repair; ability to read and interpret plans and sketches; knowledge of the proper proportions of concrete and mortar mixes; knowledge of proper and safe working practices and effective use of tools; and other related areas.

HOW TO TAKE A TEST

I. YOU MUST PASS AN EXAMINATION

A. *WHAT EVERY CANDIDATE SHOULD KNOW*

Examination applicants often ask us for help in preparing for the written test. What can I study in advance? What kinds of questions will be asked? How will the test be given? How will the papers be graded?

As an applicant for a civil service examination, you may be wondering about some of these things. Our purpose here is to suggest effective methods of advance study and to describe civil service examinations.

Your chances for success on this examination can be increased if you know how to prepare. Those "pre-examination jitters" can be reduced if you know what to expect. You can even experience an adventure in good citizenship if you know why civil service exams are given.

B. *WHY ARE CIVIL SERVICE EXAMINATIONS GIVEN?*

Civil service examinations are important to you in two ways. As a citizen, you want public jobs filled by employees who know how to do their work. As a job seeker, you want a fair chance to compete for that job on an equal footing with other candidates. The best-known means of accomplishing this two-fold goal is the competitive examination.

Exams are widely publicized throughout the nation. They may be administered for jobs in federal, state, city, municipal, town or village governments or agencies.

Any citizen may apply, with some limitations, such as the age or residence of applicants. Your experience and education may be reviewed to see whether you meet the requirements for the particular examination. When these requirements exist, they are reasonable and applied consistently to all applicants. Thus, a competitive examination may cause you some uneasiness now, but it is your privilege and safeguard.

C. *HOW ARE CIVIL SERVICE EXAMS DEVELOPED?*

Examinations are carefully written by trained technicians who are specialists in the field known as "psychological measurement," in consultation with recognized authorities in the field of work that the test will cover. These experts recommend the subject matter areas or skills to be tested; only those knowledges or skills important to your success on the job are included. The most reliable books and source materials available are used as references. Together, the experts and technicians judge the difficulty level of the questions.

Test technicians know how to phrase questions so that the problem is clearly stated. Their ethics do not permit "trick" or "catch" questions. Questions may have been tried out on sample groups, or subjected to statistical analysis, to determine their usefulness.

Written tests are often used in combination with performance tests, ratings of training and experience, and oral interviews. All of these measures combine to form the best-known means of finding the right person for the right job.

II. HOW TO PASS THE WRITTEN TEST

A. NATURE OF THE EXAMINATION

To prepare intelligently for civil service examinations, you should know how they differ from school examinations you have taken. In school you were assigned certain definite pages to read or subjects to cover. The examination questions were quite detailed and usually emphasized memory. Civil service exams, on the other hand, try to discover your present ability to perform the duties of a position, plus your potentiality to learn these duties. In other words, a civil service exam attempts to predict how successful you will be. Questions cover such a broad area that they cannot be as minute and detailed as school exam questions.

In the public service similar kinds of work, or positions, are grouped together in one "class." This process is known as *position-classification*. All the positions in a class are paid according to the salary range for that class. One class title covers all of these positions, and they are all tested by the same examination.

B. FOUR BASIC STEPS

1) Study the announcement

How, then, can you know what subjects to study? Our best answer is: "Learn as much as possible about the class of positions for which you've applied." The exam will test the knowledge, skills and abilities needed to do the work.

Your most valuable source of information about the position you want is the official exam announcement. This announcement lists the training and experience qualifications. Check these standards and apply only if you come reasonably close to meeting them.

The brief description of the position in the examination announcement offers some clues to the subjects which will be tested. Think about the job itself. Review the duties in your mind. Can you perform them, or are there some in which you are rusty? Fill in the blank spots in your preparation.

Many jurisdictions preview the written test in the exam announcement by including a section called "Knowledge and Abilities Required," "Scope of the Examination," or some similar heading. Here you will find out specifically what fields will be tested.

2) Review your own background

Once you learn in general what the position is all about, and what you need to know to do the work, ask yourself which subjects you already know fairly well and which need improvement. You may wonder whether to concentrate on improving your strong areas or on building some background in your fields of weakness. When the announcement has specified "some knowledge" or "considerable knowledge," or has used adjectives like "beginning principles of..." or "advanced ... methods," you can get a clue as to the number and difficulty of questions to be asked in any given field. More questions, and hence broader coverage, would be included for those subjects which are more important in the work. Now weigh your strengths and weaknesses against the job requirements and prepare accordingly.

3) Determine the level of the position

Another way to tell how intensively you should prepare is to understand the level of the job for which you are applying. Is it the entering level? In other words, is this the position in which beginners in a field of work are hired? Or is it an intermediate or advanced level? Sometimes this is indicated by such words as "Junior" or "Senior" in the class title. Other jurisdictions use Roman numerals to designate the level – Clerk I, Clerk II, for example. The word "Supervisor" sometimes appears in the title. If the level is not indicated by the title, check the description of duties. Will you be working under very close supervision, or will you have responsibility for independent decisions in this work?

4) Choose appropriate study materials

Now that you know the subjects to be examined and the relative amount of each subject to be covered, you can choose suitable study materials. For beginning level jobs, or even advanced ones, if you have a pronounced weakness in some aspect of your training, read a modern, standard textbook in that field. Be sure it is up to date and has general coverage. Such books are normally available at your library, and the librarian will be glad to help you locate one. For entry-level positions, questions of appropriate difficulty are chosen – neither highly advanced questions, nor those too simple. Such questions require careful thought but not advanced training.

If the position for which you are applying is technical or advanced, you will read more advanced, specialized material. If you are already familiar with the basic principles of your field, elementary textbooks would waste your time. Concentrate on advanced textbooks and technical periodicals. Think through the concepts and review difficult problems in your field.

These are all general sources. You can get more ideas on your own initiative, following these leads. For example, training manuals and publications of the government agency which employs workers in your field can be useful, particularly for technical and professional positions. A letter or visit to the government department involved may result in more specific study suggestions, and certainly will provide you with a more definite idea of the exact nature of the position you are seeking.

III. KINDS OF TESTS

Tests are used for purposes other than measuring knowledge and ability to perform specified duties. For some positions, it is equally important to test ability to make adjustments to new situations or to profit from training. In others, basic mental abilities not dependent on information are essential. Questions which test these things may not appear as pertinent to the duties of the position as those which test for knowledge and information. Yet they are often highly important parts of a fair examination. For very general questions, it is almost impossible to help you direct your study efforts. What we can do is to point out some of the more common of these general abilities needed in public service positions and describe some typical questions.

1) General information

Broad, general information has been found useful for predicting job success in some kinds of work. This is tested in a variety of ways, from vocabulary lists to questions about current events. Basic background in some field of work, such as sociology or economics, may be sampled in a group of questions. Often these are principles which have become familiar to most persons through exposure rather than through formal training. It is difficult to advise you how to study for these questions; being alert to the world around you is our best suggestion.

2) Verbal ability

An example of an ability needed in many positions is verbal or language ability. Verbal ability is, in brief, the ability to use and understand words. Vocabulary and grammar tests are typical measures of this ability. Reading comprehension or paragraph interpretation questions are common in many kinds of civil service tests. You are given a paragraph of written material and asked to find its central meaning.

3) Numerical ability

Number skills can be tested by the familiar arithmetic problem, by checking paired lists of numbers to see which are alike and which are different, or by interpreting charts and graphs. In the latter test, a graph may be printed in the test booklet which you are asked to use as the basis for answering questions.

4) Observation

A popular test for law-enforcement positions is the observation test. A picture is shown to you for several minutes, then taken away. Questions about the picture test your ability to observe both details and larger elements.

5) Following directions

In many positions in the public service, the employee must be able to carry out written instructions dependably and accurately. You may be given a chart with several columns, each column listing a variety of information. The questions require you to carry out directions involving the information given in the chart.

6) Skills and aptitudes

Performance tests effectively measure some manual skills and aptitudes. When the skill is one in which you are trained, such as typing or shorthand, you can practice. These tests are often very much like those given in business school or high school courses. For many of the other skills and aptitudes, however, no short-time preparation can be made. Skills and abilities natural to you or that you have developed throughout your lifetime are being tested.

Many of the general questions just described provide all the data needed to answer the questions and ask you to use your reasoning ability to find the answers. Your best preparation for these tests, as well as for tests of facts and ideas, is to be at your physical and mental best. You, no doubt, have your own methods of getting into an exam-taking mood and keeping "in shape." The next section lists some ideas on this subject.

IV. KINDS OF QUESTIONS

Only rarely is the "essay" question, which you answer in narrative form, used in civil service tests. Civil service tests are usually of the short-answer type. Full instructions for answering these questions will be given to you at the examination. But in case this is your first experience with short-answer questions and separate answer sheets, here is what you need to know:

1) Multiple-choice Questions

Most popular of the short-answer questions is the "multiple choice" or "best answer" question. It can be used, for example, to test for factual knowledge, ability to solve problems or judgment in meeting situations found at work.

A multiple-choice question is normally one of three types—

- It can begin with an incomplete statement followed by several possible endings. You are to find the one ending which *best* completes the statement, although some of the others may not be entirely wrong.
- It can also be a complete statement in the form of a question which is answered by choosing one of the statements listed.
- It can be in the form of a problem – again you select the best answer.

Here is an example of a multiple-choice question with a discussion which should give you some clues as to the method for choosing the right answer:

When an employee has a complaint about his assignment, the action which will *best* help him overcome his difficulty is to
- A. discuss his difficulty with his coworkers
- B. take the problem to the head of the organization
- C. take the problem to the person who gave him the assignment
- D. say nothing to anyone about his complaint

In answering this question, you should study each of the choices to find which is best. Consider choice "A" – Certainly an employee may discuss his complaint with fellow employees, but no change or improvement can result, and the complaint remains unresolved. Choice "B" is a poor choice since the head of the organization probably does not know what assignment you have been given, and taking your problem to him is known as "going over the head" of the supervisor. The supervisor, or person who made the assignment, is the person who can clarify it or correct any injustice. Choice "C" is, therefore, correct. To say nothing, as in choice "D," is unwise. Supervisors have and interest in knowing the problems employees are facing, and the employee is seeking a solution to his problem.

2) True/False Questions

The "true/false" or "right/wrong" form of question is sometimes used. Here a complete statement is given. Your job is to decide whether the statement is right or wrong.

SAMPLE: A roaming cell-phone call to a nearby city costs less than a non-roaming call to a distant city.

This statement is wrong, or false, since roaming calls are more expensive.

This is not a complete list of all possible question forms, although most of the others are variations of these common types. You will always get complete directions for answering questions. Be sure you understand *how* to mark your answers – ask questions until you do.

V. RECORDING YOUR ANSWERS

Computer terminals are used more and more today for many different kinds of exams.

For an examination with very few applicants, you may be told to record your answers in the test booklet itself. Separate answer sheets are much more common. If this separate answer sheet is to be scored by machine – and this is often the case – it is highly important that you mark your answers correctly in order to get credit.

An electronic scoring machine is often used in civil service offices because of the speed with which papers can be scored. Machine-scored answer sheets must be marked with a pencil, which will be given to you. This pencil has a high graphite content which responds to the electronic scoring machine. As a matter of fact, stray dots may register as answers, so do not let your pencil rest on the answer sheet while you are pondering the correct answer. Also, if your pencil lead breaks or is otherwise defective, ask for another.

Since the answer sheet will be dropped in a slot in the scoring machine, be careful not to bend the corners or get the paper crumpled.

The answer sheet normally has five vertical columns of numbers, with 30 numbers to a column. These numbers correspond to the question numbers in your test booklet. After each number, going across the page are four or five pairs of dotted lines. These short dotted lines have small letters or numbers above them. The first two pairs may also have a "T" or "F" above the letters. This indicates that the first two pairs only are to be used if the questions are of the true-false type. If the questions are multiple choice, disregard the "T" and "F" and pay attention only to the small letters or numbers.

Answer your questions in the manner of the sample that follows:

    32. The largest city in the United States is
          A. Washington, D.C.
          B. New York City
          C. Chicago
          D. Detroit
          E. San Francisco

1) Choose the answer you think is best. (New York City is the largest, so "B" is correct.)
2) Find the row of dotted lines numbered the same as the question you are answering. (Find row number 32)
3) Find the pair of dotted lines corresponding to the answer. (Find the pair of lines under the mark "B.")
4) Make a solid black mark between the dotted lines.

VI. BEFORE THE TEST

Common sense will help you find procedures to follow to get ready for an examination. Too many of us, however, overlook these sensible measures. Indeed, nervousness and fatigue have been found to be the most serious reasons why applicants fail to do their best on civil service tests. Here is a list of reminders:

- Begin your preparation early – Don't wait until the last minute to go scurrying around for books and materials or to find out what the position is all about.
- Prepare continuously – An hour a night for a week is better than an all-night cram session. This has been definitely established. What is more, a night a week for a month will return better dividends than crowding your study into a shorter period of time.
- Locate the place of the exam – You have been sent a notice telling you when and where to report for the examination. If the location is in a different town or otherwise unfamiliar to you, it would be well to inquire the best route and learn something about the building.
- Relax the night before the test – Allow your mind to rest. Do not study at all that night. Plan some mild recreation or diversion; then go to bed early and get a good night's sleep.
- Get up early enough to make a leisurely trip to the place for the test – This way unforeseen events, traffic snarls, unfamiliar buildings, etc. will not upset you.
- Dress comfortably – A written test is not a fashion show. You will be known by number and not by name, so wear something comfortable.
- Leave excess paraphernalia at home – Shopping bags and odd bundles will get in your way. You need bring only the items mentioned in the official notice you received; usually everything you need is provided. Do not bring reference books to the exam. They will only confuse those last minutes and be taken away from you when in the test room.
- Arrive somewhat ahead of time – If because of transportation schedules you must get there very early, bring a newspaper or magazine to take your mind off yourself while waiting.
- Locate the examination room – When you have found the proper room, you will be directed to the seat or part of the room where you will sit. Sometimes you are given a sheet of instructions to read while you are waiting. Do not fill out any forms until you are told to do so; just read them and be prepared.
- Relax and prepare to listen to the instructions
- If you have any physical problem that may keep you from doing your best, be sure to tell the test administrator. If you are sick or in poor health, you really cannot do your best on the exam. You can come back and take the test some other time.

VII. AT THE TEST

The day of the test is here and you have the test booklet in your hand. The temptation to get going is very strong. Caution! There is more to success than knowing the right answers. You must know how to identify your papers and understand variations in the type of short-answer question used in this particular examination. Follow these suggestions for maximum results from your efforts:

1) Cooperate with the monitor

The test administrator has a duty to create a situation in which you can be as much at ease as possible. He will give instructions, tell you when to begin, check to see that you are marking your answer sheet correctly, and so on. He is not there to guard you, although he will see that your competitors do not take unfair advantage. He wants to help you do your best.

2) Listen to all instructions

Don't jump the gun! Wait until you understand all directions. In most civil service tests you get more time than you need to answer the questions. So don't be in a hurry. Read each word of instructions until you clearly understand the meaning. Study the examples, listen to all announcements and follow directions. Ask questions if you do not understand what to do.

3) Identify your papers

Civil service exams are usually identified by number only. You will be assigned a number; you must not put your name on your test papers. Be sure to copy your number correctly. Since more than one exam may be given, copy your exact examination title.

4) Plan your time

Unless you are told that a test is a "speed" or "rate of work" test, speed itself is usually not important. Time enough to answer all the questions will be provided, but this does not mean that you have all day. An overall time limit has been set. Divide the total time (in minutes) by the number of questions to determine the approximate time you have for each question.

5) Do not linger over difficult questions

If you come across a difficult question, mark it with a paper clip (useful to have along) and come back to it when you have been through the booklet. One caution if you do this – be sure to skip a number on your answer sheet as well. Check often to be sure that you have not lost your place and that you are marking in the row numbered the same as the question you are answering.

6) Read the questions

Be sure you know what the question asks! Many capable people are unsuccessful because they failed to *read* the questions correctly.

7) Answer all questions

Unless you have been instructed that a penalty will be deducted for incorrect answers, it is better to guess than to omit a question.

8) Speed tests

It is often better NOT to guess on speed tests. It has been found that on timed tests people are tempted to spend the last few seconds before time is called in marking answers at random – without even reading them – in the hope of picking up a few extra points. To discourage this practice, the instructions may warn you that your score will be "corrected" for guessing. That is, a penalty will be applied. The incorrect answers will be deducted from the correct ones, or some other penalty formula will be used.

9) Review your answers

If you finish before time is called, go back to the questions you guessed or omitted to give them further thought. Review other answers if you have time.

10) Return your test materials

If you are ready to leave before others have finished or time is called, take ALL your materials to the monitor and leave quietly. Never take any test material with you. The monitor can discover whose papers are not complete, and taking a test booklet may be grounds for disqualification.

VIII. EXAMINATION TECHNIQUES

1) Read the general instructions carefully. These are usually printed on the first page of the exam booklet. As a rule, these instructions refer to the timing of the examination; the fact that you should not start work until the signal and must stop work at a signal, etc. If there are any *special* instructions, such as a choice of questions to be answered, make sure that you note this instruction carefully.

2) When you are ready to start work on the examination, that is as soon as the signal has been given, read the instructions to each question booklet, underline any key words or phrases, such as *least, best, outline, describe* and the like. In this way you will tend to answer as requested rather than discover on reviewing your paper that you *listed without describing*, that you selected the *worst* choice rather than the *best* choice, etc.

3) If the examination is of the objective or multiple-choice type – that is, each question will also give a series of possible answers: A, B, C or D, and you are called upon to select the best answer and write the letter next to that answer on your answer paper – it is advisable to start answering each question in turn. There may be anywhere from 50 to 100 such questions in the three or four hours allotted and you can see how much time would be taken if you read through all the questions before beginning to answer any. Furthermore, if you come across a question or group of questions which you know would be difficult to answer, it would undoubtedly affect your handling of all the other questions.

4) If the examination is of the essay type and contains but a few questions, it is a moot point as to whether you should read all the questions before starting to answer any one. Of course, if you are given a choice – say five out of seven and the like – then it is essential to read all the questions so you can eliminate the two that are most difficult. If, however, you are asked to answer all the questions, there may be danger in trying to answer the easiest one first because you may find that you will spend too much time on it. The best technique is to answer the first question, then proceed to the second, etc.

5) Time your answers. Before the exam begins, write down the time it started, then add the time allowed for the examination and write down the time it must be completed, then divide the time available somewhat as follows:

- If 3-1/2 hours are allowed, that would be 210 minutes. If you have 80 objective-type questions, that would be an average of 2-1/2 minutes per question. Allow yourself no more than 2 minutes per question, or a total of 160 minutes, which will permit about 50 minutes to review.
- If for the time allotment of 210 minutes there are 7 essay questions to answer, that would average about 30 minutes a question. Give yourself only 25 minutes per question so that you have about 35 minutes to review.

6) The most important instruction is to *read each question* and make sure you know what is wanted. The second most important instruction is to *time yourself properly* so that you answer every question. The third most important instruction is to *answer every question*. Guess if you have to but include something for each question. Remember that you will receive no credit for a blank and will probably receive some credit if you write something in answer to an essay question. If you guess a letter – say "B" for a multiple-choice question – you may have guessed right. If you leave a blank as an answer to a multiple-choice question, the examiners may respect your feelings but it will not add a point to your score. Some exams may penalize you for wrong answers, so in such cases *only*, you may not want to guess unless you have some basis for your answer.

7) Suggestions
    a. Objective-type questions
        1. Examine the question booklet for proper sequence of pages and questions
        2. Read all instructions carefully
        3. Skip any question which seems too difficult; return to it after all other questions have been answered
        4. Apportion your time properly; do not spend too much time on any single question or group of questions
        5. Note and underline key words – *all, most, fewest, least, best, worst, same, opposite*, etc.
        6. Pay particular attention to negatives
        7. Note unusual option, e.g., unduly long, short, complex, different or similar in content to the body of the question
        8. Observe the use of "hedging" words – *probably, may, most likely*, etc.
        9. Make sure that your answer is put next to the same number as the question
        10. Do not second-guess unless you have good reason to believe the second answer is definitely more correct
        11. Cross out original answer if you decide another answer is more accurate; do not erase until you are ready to hand your paper in
        12. Answer all questions; guess unless instructed otherwise
        13. Leave time for review

    b. Essay questions
        1. Read each question carefully
        2. Determine exactly what is wanted. Underline key words or phrases.
        3. Decide on outline or paragraph answer

4. Include many different points and elements unless asked to develop any one or two points or elements
5. Show impartiality by giving pros and cons unless directed to select one side only
6. Make and write down any assumptions you find necessary to answer the questions
7. Watch your English, grammar, punctuation and choice of words
8. Time your answers; don't crowd material

8) Answering the essay question

Most essay questions can be answered by framing the specific response around several key words or ideas. Here are a few such key words or ideas:

M's: manpower, materials, methods, money, management
P's: purpose, program, policy, plan, procedure, practice, problems, pitfalls, personnel, public relations
  a. Six basic steps in handling problems:
    1. Preliminary plan and background development
    2. Collect information, data and facts
    3. Analyze and interpret information, data and facts
    4. Analyze and develop solutions as well as make recommendations
    5. Prepare report and sell recommendations
    6. Install recommendations and follow up effectiveness

  b. Pitfalls to avoid
    1. *Taking things for granted* – A statement of the situation does not necessarily imply that each of the elements is necessarily true; for example, a complaint may be invalid and biased so that all that can be taken for granted is that a complaint has been registered
    2. *Considering only one side of a situation* – Wherever possible, indicate several alternatives and then point out the reasons you selected the best one
    3. *Failing to indicate follow up* – Whenever your answer indicates action on your part, make certain that you will take proper follow-up action to see how successful your recommendations, procedures or actions turn out to be
    4. *Taking too long in answering any single question* – Remember to time your answers properly

IX. AFTER THE TEST

Scoring procedures differ in detail among civil service jurisdictions although the general principles are the same. Whether the papers are hand-scored or graded by machine we have described, they are nearly always graded by number. That is, the person who marks the paper knows only the number – never the name – of the applicant. Not until all the papers have been graded will they be matched with names. If other tests, such as training and experience or oral interview ratings have been given, scores will be combined. Different parts of the examination usually have different weights. For example, the written test might count 60 percent of the final grade, and a rating of training and experience 40 percent. In many jurisdictions, veterans will have a certain number of points added to their grades.

After the final grade has been determined, the names are placed in grade order and an eligible list is established. There are various methods for resolving ties between those who get the same final grade – probably the most common is to place first the name of the person whose application was received first. Job offers are made from the eligible list in the order the names appear on it. You will be notified of your grade and your rank as soon as all these computations have been made. This will be done as rapidly as possible.

People who are found to meet the requirements in the announcement are called "eligibles." Their names are put on a list of eligible candidates. An eligible's chances of getting a job depend on how high he stands on this list and how fast agencies are filling jobs from the list.

When a job is to be filled from a list of eligibles, the agency asks for the names of people on the list of eligibles for that job. When the civil service commission receives this request, it sends to the agency the names of the three people highest on this list. Or, if the job to be filled has specialized requirements, the office sends the agency the names of the top three persons who meet these requirements from the general list.

The appointing officer makes a choice from among the three people whose names were sent to him. If the selected person accepts the appointment, the names of the others are put back on the list to be considered for future openings.

That is the rule in hiring from all kinds of eligible lists, whether they are for typist, carpenter, chemist, or something else. For every vacancy, the appointing officer has his choice of any one of the top three eligibles on the list. This explains why the person whose name is on top of the list sometimes does not get an appointment when some of the persons lower on the list do. If the appointing officer chooses the second or third eligible, the No. 1 eligible does not get a job at once, but stays on the list until he is appointed or the list is terminated.

X. HOW TO PASS THE INTERVIEW TEST

The examination for which you applied requires an oral interview test. You have already taken the written test and you are now being called for the interview test – the final part of the formal examination.

You may think that it is not possible to prepare for an interview test and that there are no procedures to follow during an interview. Our purpose is to point out some things you can do in advance that will help you and some good rules to follow and pitfalls to avoid while you are being interviewed.

What is an interview supposed to test?
The written examination is designed to test the technical knowledge and competence of the candidate; the oral is designed to evaluate intangible qualities, not readily measured otherwise, and to establish a list showing the relative fitness of each candidate – as measured against his competitors – for the position sought. Scoring is not on the basis of "right" and "wrong," but on a sliding scale of values ranging from "not passable" to "outstanding." As a matter of fact, it is possible to achieve a relatively low score without a single "incorrect" answer because of evident weakness in the qualities being measured.

Occasionally, an examination may consist entirely of an oral test – either an individual or a group oral. In such cases, information is sought concerning the technical knowledges and abilities of the candidate, since there has been no written examination for this purpose. More commonly, however, an oral test is used to supplement a written examination.

Who conducts interviews?

The composition of oral boards varies among different jurisdictions. In nearly all, a representative of the personnel department serves as chairman. One of the members of the board may be a representative of the department in which the candidate would work. In some cases, "outside experts" are used, and, frequently, a businessman or some other representative of the general public is asked to serve. Labor and management or other special groups may be represented. The aim is to secure the services of experts in the appropriate field.

However the board is composed, it is a good idea (and not at all improper or unethical) to ascertain in advance of the interview who the members are and what groups they represent. When you are introduced to them, you will have some idea of their backgrounds and interests, and at least you will not stutter and stammer over their names.

What should be done before the interview?

While knowledge about the board members is useful and takes some of the surprise element out of the interview, there is other preparation which is more substantive. It *is* possible to prepare for an oral interview – in several ways:

1) Keep a copy of your application and review it carefully before the interview

This may be the only document before the oral board, and the starting point of the interview. Know what education and experience you have listed there, and the sequence and dates of all of it. Sometimes the board will ask you to review the highlights of your experience for them; you should not have to hem and haw doing it.

2) Study the class specification and the examination announcement

Usually, the oral board has one or both of these to guide them. The qualities, characteristics or knowledges required by the position sought are stated in these documents. They offer valuable clues as to the nature of the oral interview. For example, if the job involves supervisory responsibilities, the announcement will usually indicate that knowledge of modern supervisory methods and the qualifications of the candidate as a supervisor will be tested. If so, you can expect such questions, frequently in the form of a hypothetical situation which you are expected to solve. NEVER go into an oral without knowledge of the duties and responsibilities of the job you seek.

3) Think through each qualification required

Try to visualize the kind of questions you would ask if you were a board member. How well could you answer them? Try especially to appraise your own knowledge and background in each area, *measured against the job sought*, and identify any areas in which you are weak. Be critical and realistic – do not flatter yourself.

4) Do some general reading in areas in which you feel you may be weak

For example, if the job involves supervision and your past experience has NOT, some general reading in supervisory methods and practices, particularly in the field of human relations, might be useful. Do NOT study agency procedures or detailed manuals. The oral board will be testing your understanding and capacity, not your memory.

5) Get a good night's sleep and watch your general health and mental attitude

You will want a clear head at the interview. Take care of a cold or any other minor ailment, and of course, no hangovers.

What should be done on the day of the interview?

Now comes the day of the interview itself. Give yourself plenty of time to get there. Plan to arrive somewhat ahead of the scheduled time, particularly if your appointment is in the fore part of the day. If a previous candidate fails to appear, the board might be ready for you a bit early. By early afternoon an oral board is almost invariably behind schedule if there are many candidates, and you may have to wait. Take along a book or magazine to read, or your application to review, but leave any extraneous material in the waiting room when you go in for your interview. In any event, relax and compose yourself.

The matter of dress is important. The board is forming impressions about you – from your experience, your manners, your attitude, and your appearance. Give your personal appearance careful attention. Dress your best, but not your flashiest. Choose conservative, appropriate clothing, and be sure it is immaculate. This is a business interview, and your appearance should indicate that you regard it as such. Besides, being well groomed and properly dressed will help boost your confidence.

Sooner or later, someone will call your name and escort you into the interview room. *This is it.* From here on you are on your own. It is too late for any more preparation. But remember, you asked for this opportunity to prove your fitness, and you are here because your request was granted.

What happens when you go in?

The usual sequence of events will be as follows: The clerk (who is often the board stenographer) will introduce you to the chairman of the oral board, who will introduce you to the other members of the board. Acknowledge the introductions before you sit down. Do not be surprised if you find a microphone facing you or a stenotypist sitting by. Oral interviews are usually recorded in the event of an appeal or other review.

Usually the chairman of the board will open the interview by reviewing the highlights of your education and work experience from your application – primarily for the benefit of the other members of the board, as well as to get the material into the record. Do not interrupt or comment unless there is an error or significant misinterpretation; if that is the case, do not hesitate. But do not quibble about insignificant matters. Also, he will usually ask you some question about your education, experience or your present job – partly to get you to start talking and to establish the interviewing "rapport." He may start the actual questioning, or turn it over to one of the other members. Frequently, each member undertakes the questioning on a particular area, one in which he is perhaps most competent, so you can expect each member to participate in the examination. Because time is limited, you may also expect some rather abrupt switches in the direction the questioning takes, so do not be upset by it. Normally, a board member will not pursue a single line of questioning unless he discovers a particular strength or weakness.

After each member has participated, the chairman will usually ask whether any member has any further questions, then will ask you if you have anything you wish to add. Unless you are expecting this question, it may floor you. Worse, it may start you off on an extended, extemporaneous speech. The board is not usually seeking more information. The question is principally to offer you a last opportunity to present further qualifications or to indicate that you have nothing to add. So, if you feel that a significant qualification or characteristic has been overlooked, it is proper to point it out in a sentence or so. Do not compliment the board on the thoroughness of their examination – they have been sketchy, and you know it. If you wish, merely say, "No thank you, I have nothing further to add." This is a point where you can "talk yourself out" of a good impression or fail to present an important bit of information. Remember, *you close the interview yourself.*

The chairman will then say, "That is all, Mr. _____, thank you." Do not be startled; the interview is over, and quicker than you think. Thank him, gather your belongings and take your leave. Save your sigh of relief for the other side of the door.

How to put your best foot forward

Throughout this entire process, you may feel that the board individually and collectively is trying to pierce your defenses, seek out your hidden weaknesses and embarrass and confuse you. Actually, this is not true. They are obliged to make an appraisal of your qualifications for the job you are seeking, and they want to see you in your best light. Remember, they must interview all candidates and a non-cooperative candidate may become a failure in spite of their best efforts to bring out his qualifications. Here are 15 suggestions that will help you:

1) Be natural – Keep your attitude confident, not cocky

If you are not confident that you can do the job, do not expect the board to be. Do not apologize for your weaknesses, try to bring out your strong points. The board is interested in a positive, not negative, presentation. Cockiness will antagonize any board member and make him wonder if you are covering up a weakness by a false show of strength.

2) Get comfortable, but don't lounge or sprawl

Sit erectly but not stiffly. A careless posture may lead the board to conclude that you are careless in other things, or at least that you are not impressed by the importance of the occasion. Either conclusion is natural, even if incorrect. Do not fuss with your clothing, a pencil or an ashtray. Your hands may occasionally be useful to emphasize a point; do not let them become a point of distraction.

3) Do not wisecrack or make small talk

This is a serious situation, and your attitude should show that you consider it as such. Further, the time of the board is limited – they do not want to waste it, and neither should you.

4) Do not exaggerate your experience or abilities

In the first place, from information in the application or other interviews and sources, the board may know more about you than you think. Secondly, you probably will not get away with it. An experienced board is rather adept at spotting such a situation, so do not take the chance.

5) If you know a board member, do not make a point of it, yet do not hide it

Certainly you are not fooling him, and probably not the other members of the board. Do not try to take advantage of your acquaintanceship – it will probably do you little good.

6) Do not dominate the interview

Let the board do that. They will give you the clues – do not assume that you have to do all the talking. Realize that the board has a number of questions to ask you, and do not try to take up all the interview time by showing off your extensive knowledge of the answer to the first one.

7) Be attentive

You only have 20 minutes or so, and you should keep your attention at its sharpest throughout. When a member is addressing a problem or question to you, give him your undivided attention. Address your reply principally to him, but do not exclude the other board members.

8) Do not interrupt

A board member may be stating a problem for you to analyze. He will ask you a question when the time comes. Let him state the problem, and wait for the question.

9) Make sure you understand the question

Do not try to answer until you are sure what the question is. If it is not clear, restate it in your own words or ask the board member to clarify it for you. However, do not haggle about minor elements.

10) Reply promptly but not hastily

A common entry on oral board rating sheets is "candidate responded readily," or "candidate hesitated in replies." Respond as promptly and quickly as you can, but do not jump to a hasty, ill-considered answer.

11) Do not be peremptory in your answers

A brief answer is proper – but do not fire your answer back. That is a losing game from your point of view. The board member can probably ask questions much faster than you can answer them.

12) Do not try to create the answer you think the board member wants

He is interested in what kind of mind you have and how it works – not in playing games. Furthermore, he can usually spot this practice and will actually grade you down on it.

13) Do not switch sides in your reply merely to agree with a board member

Frequently, a member will take a contrary position merely to draw you out and to see if you are willing and able to defend your point of view. Do not start a debate, yet do not surrender a good position. If a position is worth taking, it is worth defending.

14) Do not be afraid to admit an error in judgment if you are shown to be wrong

The board knows that you are forced to reply without any opportunity for careful consideration. Your answer may be demonstrably wrong. If so, admit it and get on with the interview.

15) Do not dwell at length on your present job

The opening question may relate to your present assignment. Answer the question but do not go into an extended discussion. You are being examined for a *new* job, not your present one. As a matter of fact, try to phrase ALL your answers in terms of the job for which you are being examined.

Basis of Rating

Probably you will forget most of these "do's" and "don'ts" when you walk into the oral interview room. Even remembering them all will not ensure you a passing grade. Perhaps you did not have the qualifications in the first place. But remembering them will help you to put your best foot forward, without treading on the toes of the board members.

Rumor and popular opinion to the contrary notwithstanding, an oral board wants you to make the best appearance possible. They know you are under pressure – but they also want to see how you respond to it as a guide to what your reaction would be under the pressures of the job you seek. They will be influenced by the degree of poise you display, the personal traits you show and the manner in which you respond.

ABOUT THIS BOOK

This book contains tests divided into Examination Sections. Go through each test, answering every question in the margin. At the end of each test look at the answer key and check your answers. On the ones you got wrong, look at the right answer choice and learn. Do not fill in the answers first. Do not memorize the questions and answers, but understand the answer and principles involved. On your test, the questions will likely be different from the samples. Questions are changed and new ones added. If you understand these past questions you should have success with any changes that arise. Tests may consist of several types of questions. We have additional books on each subject should more study be advisable or necessary for you. Finally, the more you study, the better prepared you will be. This book is intended to be the last thing you study before you walk into the examination room. Prior study of relevant texts is also recommended. NLC publishes some of these in our Fundamental Series. Knowledge and good sense are important factors in passing your exam. Good luck also helps. So now study this Passbook, absorb the material contained within and take that knowledge into the examination. Then do your best to pass that exam.

EXAMINATION SECTION

EXAMINATION SECTION

TEST 1

DIRECTIONS: Each question or incomplete statement is followed by several suggested answers or completions. Select the one that BEST answers the question or completes the statement. *PRINT THE LETTER OF THE CORRECT ANSWER IN THE SPACE AT THE RIGHT.*

Questions 1-16.

DIRECTIONS: Questions 1 through 16 are to be answered on the basis of the following tools. These tools are NOT shown to scale.

1. In order to cut a piece of 5/16" diameter steel scaffold hoisting cable, you should use tool number   1.____
    A. 6   B. 7   C. 19   D. 23

2. Scaffold planks are secured to joisting irons by means of lag screws. To properly tighten these lag screws, you should use tool number   2.____
    A. 12   B. 13   C. 20   D. 42

3. While installing a steel angle iron lintel, you find that the threads on the embedded holding bolts are damaged. You should repair the threads by using tool number   3.____
    A. 7   B. 9   C. 25   D. 43

4. It is necessary to cut a hole in a concrete foundation wall in order to place a small bolt. To cut this small hole, you should use tool number   4.____
    A. 14   B. 19   C. 21   D. 40

5. If tool number 17 bears the mark "7," this tool should be used to drill holes having a diameter of   5,____
    A. 7/64"   B. 7/32"   C. 7/16"   D. 7/8"

6. If the marking on the blade of tool number 18 reads "10-18," the "18" refers to the   6.____
    A. number of teeth per inch   B. weight
    C. thickness   D. length

7. If two points are separated by a vertical distance of 12 feet, the tool that should be used to make certain that the points are in *perfect* vertical alignment is number   7.____
    A. 11   B. 28   C. 34   D. 37

8. A ¾" diameter hole must be made in a steel floor beam. The tool you should use is number   8.____
    A. 3   B. 5   C. 9   D. 22

9. To cut the corner off a building brick, you should use tool number   9.____
    A. 4   B. 27   C. 29   D. 36

10. A 2" x 2" x ³/₁₆" steel angle should be cut using tool number   10.____
    A. 6   B. 7   C. 18   D. 19

11. The term "snips" should be applied to tool number   11.____
    A. 6   B. 13   C. 20   D. 23

12. To line-up the bolt holes in two structural steel beams, you should use tool number   12.____
    A. 1   B. 33   C. 35   D. 36

13. A "hawk" is tool number   13.____
    A. 29   B. 30   C. 38   D. 41

14. After an 8" thick brick wall has been erected, it is discovered that a hole   14.____
should have been left for a 4" sewer pipe.
To cut that hole, you should use tool number
    A. 5   B. 19   C. 32   D. 36

15. A "float" is tool number   15.____
    A. 30   B. 31   C. 33   D. 41

16. A "Stillson" is tool number   16.____
    A. 2   B. 8   C. 12   D. 22

Questions 17-33.

DIRECTIONS: Questions 17 through 33 are concerned with terms commonly used in the bricklayer trade. Answer these questions by selecting the meaning as used in the trade.

17. A "skewback" is part of a(n)   17.____
    A. column   B. beam   C. arch   D. parapet

18. A "snap header" is a   18.____
    A. bond stone   B. false header
    C. glazed brick   D. rounded bond brick

19. A "putlog" is a part of a   19.____
    A. roof   B. scaffold   C. foundation   D. ladder

20. A "corbel" is a   20.____
    A. hole   B. recess   C. projection   D. chase

21. A "reglet" is usually found in a   21.____
    A. glazed block   B. fire brick
    C. common brick   D. flashing block

22. "Efflorescence" is caused by   22.____
    A. erosion   B. expansion   C. salts   D. freezing

23. "Parging" is usually applied only to _____ walls.   23.____
    A. veneered   B. faced   C. foundation   D. hollow

24. A "salmon" brick is one that is   24.____
    A. oversized   B. glazed   C. underburned   D. overburned

25. "Centering" is used in connection with   25.____
    A. archways   B. parapets
    C. window sills   D. roof penthouses

26. A "reveal" usually occurs at
    A. windows   B. chimneys   C. parapets   D. doorways
    26._____

27. A "chase" is like a
    A. projection   B. belt course   C. recess   D. parapet
    27._____

28. "Bulking" occurs when sand is
    A. shifted   B. rammed   C. moistened   D. dried
    28._____

29. "Weep holes" are usually placed in _____ walls.
    A. solid brick   B. veneered   C. cavity   D. combination
    29._____

30. A "compass brick" is
    A. rounded on one end   B. circular
    C. square   D. wedge-shaped
    30._____

31. A "storey pole" is used with
    A. scaffolds   B. vertical distances
    C. flags   D. platforms
    31._____

32. A "dove-tail" anchor would MOST likely bond brick veneer to a _____ wall.
    A. concrete   B. cinder block
    C. wood frame   D. brick
    32._____

33. A "fore cut" is made in a
    A. column   B. joist   C. stud   D. rafter
    33._____

34. In high-rise concrete buildings, the underside of the floor slabs are frequently painted.
Before painting, the underside surfaces should be
    A. troweled   B. floated   C. screeded   D. rubbed
    34._____

35. In laying a cavity wall, a bricklayer will sometimes place a wood board on top of the ties.
The MAIN purpose for using this board is to
    A. maintain proper width of cavity   B. catch any mortar droppings
    C. aid in keeping courses level   D. properly space the ties
    35._____

36. Sometimes two different grades of brick are used in the exterior wall of a building. Face brick is used on the outside face and a backing brick is used for the inside.
The MAIN reason for this practice is
    A. speed in erection
    B. lower cost
    C. increased strength of the wall
    D. greater resistance to water penetration
    36._____

37. When cement mortar stiffens before it can be used, it is possible to make it workable once again by retempering.
    Such retempering is considered
    A. *good*, because it prevents waste of the expensive mortar
    B. *good*, because it prevents delay in the work
    C. *bad*, because it weakens the mortar
    D. *bad*, because it requires additional labor cost

37.____

38. The MAIN reason for removing nails from used lumber is that
    A. nails which are not bent can be used again
    B. workers may be injured by projecting nails
    C. the nails might rust and not be re-usable
    D. it will be easier to pile up the lumber

38.____

39. It is considered *good* practice to cut glazed brick using a(n)
    A. mason's hammer   B. abrasive wheel
    C. wide chisel   D. hacksaw

39.____

40. The MAIN purpose of adding calcium chloride to a mortar mix is to
    A. color the mortar   B. increase its workability
    C. reduce its freezing temperature   D. speed up its setting rate

40.____

_____

KEY (CORRECT ANSWERS)

1.	A	11.	D	21.	D	31.	B
2.	D	12.	C	22.	C	32.	A
3.	C	13.	B	23.	B	33.	B
4.	C	14.	D	24.	C	34.	D
5.	C	15.	D	25.	A	35.	B
6.	A	16.	C	26.	A	36.	B
7.	B	17.	C	27.	C	37.	C
8.	B	18.	B	28.	C	38.	B
9.	C	19.	B	29.	C	39.	B
10.	C	20.	C	30.	D	40.	D

_____

TEST 2

DIRECTIONS: Each question or incomplete statement is followed by several suggested answers or completions. Select the one that BEST answers the question or completes the statement. *PRINT THE LETTER OF THE CORRECT ANSWER IN THE SPACE AT THE RIGHT.*

Questions 1-8.

DIRECTIONS: Questions 1 through 16 are to be answered on the basis of the following concrete masonry units.

CONCRETE MASONRY UNITS

1. The unit that should be used for bonding with brick facing is number   1._____
   A. 2   B. 3   C. 6   D. 10

2. The unit that should be used at the side of a door opening is number   2._____
   A. 1   B. 3   C. 6   D. 11

3. The unit known as a "bull nose" is number   3._____
   A. 1   B. 8   C. 10   D. 11

4. The unit that should be used to make a lintel is number   4._____
   A. 6   B. 7   C. 9   D. 10

5. The unit that should be used at the outside corner of a wall is number   5._____
   A. 3   B. 6   C. 7   D. 8

6. The unit that should be used in a 16" square free-standing pier is number   6._____
   A. 4   B. 7   C. 8   D. 9

7. The unit known as a "stretcher" is number   7._____
   A. 4   B. 6   C. 10   D. 11

8. The unit that should be used to support a floor joist is number   8.____
    A. 2   B. 3   C. 6   D. 9

9. Cinder concrete blocks, as compared with stone concrete blocks, are   9.____
    A. heavier   B. more waterproof
    C. stronger   D. better insulators

10. The MAIN reason why a job site should be kept as neat as possible is that   10.____
this practice
    A. makes it easier to locate materials
    B. increases the availability of storage space
    C. improves morale by providing better working conditions
    D. reduces the likelihood of workers being involved in accidents

Questions 11-13.

DIRECTIONS: Questions 11 through 13 are to be answered on the basis of the sketches
                  shown at the right of each question.

11. The wall shown is a _____ wall.   11.____
    A. cavity
    B. block
    C. rowlock
    D. veneer

12. The groove which is cut in the   12.____
coping shown is a(n)
    A. caulking groove
    B. expansion joint
    C. drip
    D. expansion slot

13. The wall shown is a _____ wall.   13.____
    A. cavity
    B. block
    C. rowlock
    D. veneer

14. The MOST important factor governing the strength of a concrete mix is the ratio of cement to
    A. water
    B. gravel
    C. sand
    D. sand and gravel combined

14.____

15. The MOST important safety precaution that one should take when using a pneumatic hammer to chip concrete is to wear
    A. safety shoes
    B. goggles
    C. a long-sleeve shirt
    D. a hard hat

15.____

16. The rate at which fresh concrete hardens
    A. will increase with a rise in temperature
    B. will increase with a fall in temperature
    C. will increase with any large change in temperature
    D. is independent of the temperature

16.____

17. The MAIN reason why re-bars should NOT be painted is that the paint will
    A. be removed when the concrete is poured
    B. reduce the bond between the concrete and the steel
    C. not be seen since the re-bars are buried in the concrete
    D. greatly increase the cost

17.____

Questions 18-23.

DIRECTIONS: Questions 18 through 23 are to be answered on the basis of the following mortar joints.

    1   2   3   4   5   6

MORTAR JOINTS

18. A raked joint is number
    A. 1   B. 2   C. 3   D. 4

18.____

19. A V joint is number
    A. 3   B. 4   C. 5   D. 6

19.____

20. A flush joint is number
    A. 1   B. 2   C. 3   D. 4

20.____

21. A weather joint is number   21.____
    A. 3   B. 4   C. 5   D. 6

22. A struck joint is number   22.____
    A. 1   B. 2   C. 3   D. 4

23. A concave joint is number   23.____
    A. 1   B. 3   C. 4   D. 6

Questions 24-28.

DIRECTIONS: Questions 24 through 28 are to be answered on the basis of the following
              pattern bonds.

1

2

3

4

5

PATTERN BONDS

6

24. Common bond is number   24.____
    A. 1   B. 2   C. 3   D. 4

25. Stack bond is number   25.____
    A. 3   B. 4   C. 5   D. 6

26. English bond is number   26.____
    A. 1   B. 2   C. 3   D. 4

27. Flemish bond is number   27.____
    A. 1   B. 2   C. 3   D. 4

28. Running bond is number   28.____
    A. 1   B. 3   C. 5   D. 6

29. Recently poured concrete sidewalks are frequently covered with building   29.____
    paper MAINLY to
    A. absorb the excess water from the surface
    B. make the concrete set more uniformly
    C. prevent pedestrians from walking on it
    D. protect the concrete from wind-blown dust and dirt

30. The practice of oiling forms prior to placing concrete is considered   30._____
    A. *poor*, since oil may get on the rods
    B. *poor*, since this discolors the concrete surface
    C. *good*, since this makes the concrete flow better
    D. *good*, since this makes stripping easier

_____

KEY (CORRECT ANSWERS)

1.	A	11.	A	21.	D
2.	D	12.	C	22.	B
3.	C	13.	D	23.	C
4.	A	14.	A	24.	B
5.	D	15.	B	25.	D
6.	D	16.	A	26.	D
7.	A	17.	B	27.	C
8.	B	18.	C	28.	A
9.	D	19.	C	29.	B
10.	D	20.	A	30.	D

_____

EXAMINATION SECTION
TEST 1

DIRECTIONS: Each question or incomplete statement is followed by several suggested answers or completions. Select the one that BEST answers the question or completes the statement. *PRINT THE LETTER OF THE CORRECT ANSWER IN THE SPACE AT THE RIGHT.*

1. A *flashed* or *flare* header is a

    A. dark-colored brick   B. light-colored brick
    C. bat   D. full-sized brick

1.____

2. A brick apron wall would MOST likely be used with

    A. wood frame construction   B. steel frame construction
    C. masonry bearing walls   D. none of the above

2.____

3. According to the building code, a hollow wall is built

    A. with hollow masonry units
    B. with solid masonry units
    C. without mortar
    D. to form interior walls only

3.____

4. The brick veneer of masonry wall is

    A. not joined to the wall in any way
    B. bonded to the wall
    C. tied to the wall
    D. separated from the wall by an appreciable air space

4.____

5. Increasing the amount of sand in a mortar for masonry will result in a mortar which is

    A. stronger   B. more water resistant
    C. lower in shrinkage   D. slower setting

5.____

6. Retempering of mortar is permissible

    A. with cement mortar   B. with lime mortar
    C. with cement-lime mortar   D. in no case

6.____

7. The frog in a brick

    A. is an imperfection
    B. is a trademark
    C. increases the weight of the brick
    D. provides a key for mortar

7.____

8. The MOST likely use of snap headers in an 8-inch brick wall is to

    A. improve the appearance of the wall
    B. increase the strength of the wall
    C. reduce the quantity of face brick in the wall
    D. simplify the laying of the brick

8.____

9. After a brick wall is completed, it is to be washed with a solution of muriatic acid. Washing is to be done from a swinging scaffold. The scaffold should be supported by   9.____

    A. manila rope   B. hemp rope
    C. steel cables   D. wrought iron chain

10. Before washing a brick wall with acid, mortar adhering to the face of the wall should be removed by using a   10.____

    A. stiff brush and a carborundum stone
    B. hammer
    C. hammer and chisel
    D. wooden mallet

11. In applying muriatic acid solution to a brick wall, the bricklayer should use a(n) _____ _____ pail and _____ brush.   11.____

    A. iron; wire   B. wooden; fiber
    C. wooden; wire   D. iron; fiber

12. A wood float is used to finish concrete surfaces when   12.____

    A. a smooth but gritty surface is desired
    B. a rough surface is desired
    C. a very smooth surface is desired
    D. the concrete mix is very stiff

13. Troweling of concrete should be done   13.____

    A. immediately after the concrete is struck off in the forms
    B. just before the concrete mix shows any stiffness
    C. after the concrete is stiff enough to walk on
    D. when the concrete is quite stiff but still workable

14. *Curing* of concrete is important   14.____

    A. if the mix is very wet
    B. if the mix is very dry
    C. regardless of the water-cement ratio of the mix
    D. in cold weather only

15. A mortar mix is called a 1:1:6 mix. The numbers refer to the following ingredients of the mortar: 15.____

    A. cement, water, and sand
    B. cement, lime, and sand
    C. cement, sand, and gravel
    D. lime, water, and sand

16. Mortar droppings inside a cavity wall are   16.____

    A. good because they strengthen the wall
    B. bad because they may block weep holes
    C. good because they make the wall more resistant to the passage of water
    D. bad because they prevent air circulation within the wall

Questions 17-21.

DIRECTIONS: Questions 17 through 21, inclusive, refer to the concrete masonry units shown in the sketches below.

17. Of the above units, the one which would be used at the intersection of two walls is num-   17._____
     bered

     A. 2   B. 5   C. 8   D. 11

18. Of the above units, the one which would be used as a header is numbered   18._____

     A. 1   B. 3   C. 4   D. 6

19. Of the above units, the one which would be used to form the sides of a door opening is   19._____
     numbered

     A. 1   B. 2   C. 4   D. 5

20. The unit which would be used in connection with steel reinforcement in a wall is num-   20._____
     bered

     A. 1   B. 6   C. 9   D. 11

21. The unit which would be used in cavity wall construction is numbered   21._____

     A. 7   B. 8   C. 10   D. 11

22. A pail with a volume of one cubic foot holds exactly 7.48 gallons of water. A gallon of   22._____
     water occupies a space, in cubic inches, of

     A. 227   B. 229   C. 231   D. 233

23. A bullnose brick would MOST likely be used   23._____

     A. in arch work   B. for window sills
     C. for backing   D. for chimneys

13

24. Camber would MOST likely be found in   24.____

    A.   solid brick walls   B.   cavity walls of brick
    C.   wooden joists   D.   steel columns

25. Centering would MOST likely be used in the construction of brick   25.____

    A.   arches   B.   sidewalks
    C.   walls   D.   all of the above

26. A closer or closure brick is   26.____

    A.   the last brick placed in a brick structure
    B.   a brick adjoining a door or window opening in a wall
    C.   a brick used to form the intersection of two walls
    D.   the last brick placed in a course of brick work

27. Firebrick would be LEAST likely to be used in   27.____

    A.   fire walls   B.   flues
    C.   fireplaces   D.   furnace linings

28. A lewis is generally used to lift   28.____

    A.   stone   B.   brick
    C.   concrete block   D.   wood

29. The opposite of batter is   29.____

    A.   camber   B.   miter   C.   chamfer   D.   overhang

30. The term *withe* or *wythe* is used in connection with   30.____

    A.   floors   B.   spandrels   C.   walls   D.   openings

31. A lead in bricklaying corresponds in function MOST closely to   31.____

    A.   a ground in plastering
    B.   flashing in roofing
    C.   a miter in carpentry
    D.   a float in concrete work

32. Terra cotta tile which is usually scored so that it can be split easily on the job is USUALLY   32.____
intended for

    A.   backup work   B.   tile bearing walls
    C.   tile partitions   D.   furring

33. A 12-inch brick wall built with standard (not modular) brick is actually 12 1/4 inches thick.   33.____
The thickness of the mortar joint between a stretcher on one face of the wall and a
header on the other is, in inches, MOST NEARLY

    A.   1/4   B.   3/8   C.   1/2   D.   5/8

34. Assume a 2 x 4 is 12'6" long. The number of board feet in this 2 x 4 is MOST NEARLY   34.____

    A.   7.9   B.   8.1   C.   8.3   D.   8.5

35. The sum of 5/12 and 1/4 is   35.____

    A. 7/12   B. 2/3   C. 3/4   D. 5/6

36. In brickwork, the terms *raked, struck,* and *weathered* refer to the   36.____

    A. bond   B. type of mortar
    C. type of brick   D. type of pointing

37. The furrow in the mortar of a bed joint should be   37.____

    A. deep   B. shallow
    C. wide   D. prohibited

38. Assume the masonry facing of a veneered wall is connected to the wall by dovetail anchors. The wall is MOST likely made of   38.____

    A. concrete   B. wood
    C. stone masonry   D. terra cotta tile

39. Upon opening a bag of cement, many lumps are found which cannot be crumbled by hand. The BEST thing to do in this case is   39.____

    A. sieve the cement to remove the lumps
    B. break up the lumps with a hammer
    C. use the cement as is but use more of it than would otherwise be used
    D. discard this bag and all others like it

40. In reinforced concrete work, wire chairs are GENERALLY used to   40.____

    A. reinforce sharp corners
    B. reinforce concrete in the interior of the member
    C. position reinforcing rods
    D. tie reinforcing rods together

KEY (CORRECT ANSWERS)

1.	A	11.	B	21.	C	31.	A
2.	B	12.	A	22.	C	32.	D
3.	B	13.	D	23.	B	33.	C
4.	C	14.	C	24.	C	34.	C
5.	C	15.	B	25.	A	35.	B
6.	B	16.	B	26.	D	36.	D
7.	D	17.	A	27.	A	37.	B
8.	C	18.	B	28.	A	38.	A
9.	C	19.	D	29.	D	39.	D
10.	A	20.	D	30.	C	40.	C

TEST 2

DIRECTIONS: Each question or incomplete statement is followed by several suggested answers or completions. Select the one that BEST answers the question or completes the statement. *PRINT THE LETTER OF THE CORRECT ANSWER IN THE SPACE AT THE RIGHT.*

1. The foundation for a brick wall should be at least four feet below ground surface. A shallower depth would be UNSATISFACTORY because   1.____

   A. the bearing value of the soil would be too small
   B. the foundation would be above the frost line
   C. the wall would not provide adequate insulation for the building
   D. burrowing animals could dig under the wall

2. In concrete work, wooden form spreaders   2.____

   A. are never removed
   B. should be removed before they are covered with concrete
   C. should be removed after they are well covered with concrete
   D. should be removed after the concrete has taken its initial set

3. Concrete for a 6-inch reinforced concrete wall has a slump of 2 inches. The defect that would MOST likely be found in the finished wall would be   3.____

   A. honeycombing   B. segregation
   C. excessive laitance   D. improper curing

4. Within practical limits, the MOST important factor governing the strength of a concrete mix is the ratio of cement to   4.____

   A. sand   B. gravel
   C. sand and gravel   D. water

5. A plan view of a building would be the BEST view to refer to in order to determine   5.____

   A. details of bond in a wall
   B. story height
   C. clear spacing between walls
   D. height of parapet

6. The interior surfaces of concrete form work are coated with oil PRIMARILY to   6.____

   A. provide concrete with smooth surfaces
   B. prevent honeycombing
   C. make form removal easier
   D. aid in curing the concrete

7. The volume of earth, in cubic yards, excavated from a trench 4' 0" wide by 5' 6" deep by 18' 6" long is MOST NEARLY   7.____

   A. 14.7   B. 15.1   C. 15.5   D. 15.9

8. A deformed bar used as reinforcement in reinforced concrete USUALLY   8.____

    A. is a twisted rod
    B. is bent at one or both ends
    C. has a different shape than the other bars in the pour
    D. has projecting lugs

9. The PRIMARY objection to continued troweling of a concrete floor when a smooth finish   9.____
is desired is that such a practice

    A. makes a very slippery floor
    B. increases the cost
    C. produces a surface which will chalk or dust
    D. brings the coarse aggregate to the surface

10. When a chute is used to deposit concrete for a floor, the LEAST important consideration   10.____
in placing the chute is

    A. the height of the discharge end above the floor
    B. the slope of the chute
    C. making provision to move the discharge end to any spot on the floor
    D. the sharpness of the angle where the chute changes direction horizontally

11. Beveled chamfer strips are used in the construction of formwork for concrete to   11.____

    A. eliminate right-angle corners in the forms
    B. make the forms watertight
    C. strengthen the forms
    D. position reinforcing bars

12. In reinforced concrete work, steel reinforcing bars USUALLY are   12.____

    A. bent at the steel mill
    B. heated to a red heat before bending on the job
    C. cut and welded on the job to form bends
    D. bent cold on a bar bending table

13. Of the following structural steel shapes, the one which would MOST likely be used for the   13.____
lintel of a standard window in a brick wall is

    A. ⊥   B. ⊐   C. ⌐L   D. ⌐

14. In a pile of enameled brick, it would be very unusual to find a brick which was glazed on   14.____
more than the following number of faces:

    A. 1   B. 2   C. 3   D. 4

15. To cut glazed brick,   15.____

    A. the identical method is used as in cutting common brick
    B. a power saw must be used
    C. a rotating abrasive disk should be used
    D. a hammer and chisel should be used

16. A bricklayer's level is placed on a flat surface which is apparently horizontal. The bubble is displaced one mark to the right. When the level is replaced on the surface with the ends of the level reversed, the bubble is again displaced one mark to the right. This indicates that

    A. the surface is horizontal
    B. the bubble tube is not set properly
    C. the bubble tube is set properly
    D. it is necessary to test the level on a known horizontal surface before any conclusion can be reached

16.____

17. The first course of a lead consists of three bricks. The height of this lead, in courses, would normally be

    A. 7   B. 6   C. 3   D. 4

17.____

18. Assume a wall consists of face brick and back-up tile. Before back-plastering the face brick (before the back-up units are laid), the joints in the back of the face brick should be

    A. cut flush   B. left as is
    C. carefully tooled   D. raked

18.____

19. Spalls would MOST probably be used by a

    A. carpenter   B. bricklayer
    C. stone mason   D. concrete worker

19.____

20. Tooling of face joints in brick work should be done

    A. after a course is completed
    B. immediately after laying four or five bricks
    C. after the mortar has acquired its initial set
    D. after the mortar has acquired its final set

20.____

21. A slump test would MOST likely be performed by a

    A. bricklayer   B. concrete worker
    C. carpenter   D. plumber

21.____

22. In brick work, a course consisting of brick set on end is known as _____ course.

    A. rowlock   B. belt   C. lacing   D. soldier

22.____

23. The same type of mortar would be used on all of the following units EXCEPT

    A. common brick   B. glazed brick
    C. fire brick   D. concrete block

23.____

24. Stone concrete block is inferior to cinder concrete block in

    A. strength   B. appearance
    C. durability   D. insulation

24.____

25. A coping is USUALLY held in place by

    A. mortar   B. nails   C. bolts   D. rivets

25.____

26. As used by bricklayers, *culling* is a terra used when   26.____

    A. cutting block to size
    B. selecting good brick from a pile
    C. making a furrow in the mortar bed
    D. laying the first brick in a wall

27. To obtain <u>durability</u>, exposed brickwork should be built of well-burned bricks. As used in   27.____
the above sentence, <u>durability</u> means MOST NEARLY

    A. beauty   B. water resistance
    C. strength   D. long life

28. A common mistake is to <u>assume</u> that the strength of masonry is the most important fac-   28.____
tor. As used in the above sentence, <u>assume</u> means MOST NEARLY

    A. determine   B. take for granted
    C. figure   D. make sure

29. To produce a <u>more plastic</u> mortar, lime putty is added to cement mortar. As used in the   29.____
above sentence, <u>more plastic</u> means MOST NEARLY

    A. whiter   B. easier to work
    C. smoother   D. denser

30. Copings should be made of <u>impervious</u> materials. As used in the above sentence, <u>imper-</u>   30.____
<u>vious</u> means MOST NEARLY

    A. solid   B. expensive
    C. water resistant   D. strong

31. A steak weighed 2 pounds 4 ounces. How much did it cost at $4.60 per pound?   31.____

    A. $7.80   B. $8.75   C. $9.90   D. $10.35

32. During his summer vacation, a boy earned $45.00 per day and saved 60% of his earn-   32.____
ings. If he worked 45 days, how much did he save during his vacation?

    A. $15.00   B. $18.00   C. $1215.00   D. $22.50

33. From his coin bank, a boy took 3 half dollars, 8 quarters, 7 dimes, 6 nickels, and 9 pen-   33.____
nies to deposit in his school savings account. Express in dollars and cents the total
amount of money he deposited.

    A. $2.82   B. $4.59   C. $6.42   D. $7.52

34. If a roast that requires 1 hour and 40 minutes of roasting time has been in the oven for 55   34.____
minutes, how many more minutes of roasting time are required?

    A. 30   B. 36   C. 45   D. 55

35. On the first day of its drive, a school raised $400, which was 33 1/3% of its Red Cross   35.____
quota. How much was the quota?

    A. $1,200   B. $1,300   C. $1,400   D. $1,500

36. On a certain map, a distance of 10 miles is represented by 1/2 inch. If two towns are 3 1/ 2 inches apart on this map, express in miles the actual distance between the two towns.   36._____

    A. 70   B. 80   C. 90   D. 100

37. At an annual rate of $.40 per $100, what is the fire insurance premium for one year on a house that is insured for $80,000?   37._____

    A. $120   B. $160   C. $240   D. $320

38. A meter equals approximately 1.09 yards. How much longer, in yards, is a 100-meter dash than a 100-yard dash?   38._____

    A. 6   B. 8   C. 9   D. 12

39. A train leaves New York City at 8:10 A.M. and arrives in Buffalo at 4:45 P.M. on the same day. How long, in hours and minutes, does it take the train to make the trip?
_____ hours, _____ minutes.   39._____

    A. 6; 22   B. 7; 16   C. 7; 28   D. 8; 35

40. A jacket that was marked at $125.00 was sold for $100. What was the rate of discount on the marked price?   40._____

    A. 10%   B. 15%   C. 18%   D. 20%

KEY (CORRECT ANSWERS)

1.	B	11.	A	21.	B	31.	D
2.	B	12.	D	22.	D	32.	C
3.	A	13.	C	23.	C	33.	B
4.	D	14.	B	24.	D	34.	C
5.	C	15.	C	25.	A	35.	A
6.	C	16.	C	26.	B	36.	A
7.	B	17.	B	27.	D	37.	D
8.	D	18.	A	28.	B	38.	C
9.	C	19.	C	29.	B	39.	D
10.	D	20.	C	30.	C	40.	D

EXAMINATION SECTION
TEST 1

DIRECTIONS: Each question or incomplete statement is followed by several suggested answers or completions. Select the one that BEST answers the question or completes the statement. *PRINT THE LETTER OF THE CORRECT ANSWER IN THE SPACE AT THE RIGHT.*

1. Concrete with a slump of 2 inches would *most likely* be used for   1.____

    A. floors   B. thin wall sections
    C. columns   D. deep beams

2. The structure above the roof of a building which encloses a stairway is called a   2.____

    A. scuttle   B. bulkhead
    C. penthouse   D. shaft

3. A #4 reinforcing bar has a diameter, in inches, of *approximately*   3.____

    A. 1/4   B. 3/8   C. 1/2   D. 5/8

4. A spandrel beam will usually be found   4.____

    A. at the wall   B. around stairs
    C. at the peak of a roof   D. underneath a column

5. Oil is applied to the inside surfaces of concrete forms to   5.____

    A. prevent loss of water from the concrete
    B. obtain smoother concrete surfaces
    C. make stripping easier
    D. prevent honeycombing

6. A retaining wall is built with a batter.
Of the following conditions, the one which *most likely* applies to the wall is   6.____

    A. it is out of plumb
    B. it is thinner at top than at bottom
    C. neither surface is vertical
    D. both surfaces are vertical

7. Two cubic yards of sand and four cubic yards of broken stone are to be used to make 1:2:4 concrete.
If all the aggregate is used, the number of bags of cement that would be required is   7.____

    A. 1   B. 9   C. 18   D. 27

8. A rectangular plot is 30 feet wide by 60 feet long. The length of the diagonal, in feet, is *most nearly*   8.____

    A. 68   B. 67   C. 66   D. 65

9. Wood floor joists are supported on masonry walls which have a clear spacing of 17'0". The number of rows of cross-bridging required is   9.____

    A. 4   B. 3   C. 2   D. 1

10. When painting wood, the puttying of nail holes and cracks should be done   10.____

    A. *after* the priming coat is dry
    B. *before* the priming coat is applied
    C. *while* the priming coat is still wet
    D. *after* the finish coat is applied

11. The material that would normally be used to make a corbel in a brick wall is   11.____

    A. brick   B. wood   C. steel   D. concrete

12. Headers and trimmers are used in the construction of   12.____

    A. footings   B. walls   C. floors   D. arches

13. In the design of stairs, the designer should consider   13.____

    A. maximum height of riser only
    B. minimum width of tread only
    C. product of riser height by tread width only
    D. all of the above

14. A reduction in the required number of columns in a building can be made by using one of the following types of beam. Which one?   14.____

    A. floor   B. girder   C. cantilever   D. jack

15. Doors sheathed in metal are known as _____ doors.   15.____

    A. kalamein   B. tin-clad   C. bethlehem   D. flemish

16. A coat of plaster which is scratched deliberately would *most likely* be   16.____

    A. used in two-coat work only
    B. the first coat placed
    C. the second coat placed
    D. condemned by the inspector

17. A concealed draft opening is   17.____

    A. *good* because it improves the appearance of a room
    B. *bad* because it might be accidentally blocked up
    C. *good* because it can be used to regulate the flow of fresh air
    D. *bad* because it is a fire hazard

18. A groove is cut in the underside of a stone sill.
This is done to   18.____

    A. keep rain water from running down the wall
    B. allow the insertion of dowels
    C. improve the mortar bond
    D. reduce the weight of the sill

19. Of the following, the one which would LEAST likely be used in conjunction with the others is

19.____

    A. rafter
    B. collar beam
    C. ridgeboard
    D. tail beam

20. The dimensions of a 2 x 4 when dressed are, *most nearly*,

20.____

    A. 2 x 4
    B. 1 1/2 x 3 1/2
    C. 1 5/8 x 3 5/8
    D. 1 3/4 x 3 1/2

21. The story heights of a building could be MOST readily determined from

21.____

    A. a plan view
    B. an elevation view
    C. a plot map
    D. all of the above

22. Honeycombing in concrete is *most likely* to occur

22.____

    A. if the forms are vibrated
    B. near the top of the forms
    C. if the mix is stiff
    D. if the concrete is well-spaded

23. A weather joint in brick work is one in which the mortar is

23.____

    A. flush with the face of the lower brick and slopes inward
    B. flush with the face of the upper brick and slopes inward
    C. recessed a fixed distance behind the face of the brick
    D. flush with the face of upper and lower brick but curves inward between the two bricks

24. A 12 inch brick wall is constructed using stretchers only.
The PRINCIPAL objection to such a wall is with

24.____

    A. appearance
    B. construction difficulties
    C. bond
    D. dimensional problems

25. To prevent sagging joists from damaging a brick wall in the event of a fire, it is BEST to

25.____

    A. anchor the joists firmly in the wall
    B. make a bevel cut on the end of the joists
    C. use bridal irons to support the joists
    D. box out the wall for the joists

26. Flashing would *most likely* be found in a

26.____

    A. footing
    B. floor
    C. ceiling
    D. parapet

27. Vermiculite is used in plaster to

27.____

    A. reduce weight
    B. permit easier cleaning
    C. give architectural effects
    D. reduce the mixing water required

28. The volume in cubic feet of a room 8'6" wide by 10'6" long by 8'8" high is *most nearly*   28.____

    A. 770   B. 774   C. 778   D. 782

29. A slab of concrete is 2'0" by 3'0" by 8" thick.
The weight of the slab is, in pounds, *most nearly*   29.____

    A. 450   B. 500   C. 550   D. 600

30. Wainscoting is USUALLY found on   30.____

    A. floors   B. walls   C. ceilings   D. roofs

31. A piece of wood covering the plaster below the stool of a window is called a(n)   31.____

    A. apron   B. sill   C. coping   D. trimmer

32. English bond is used in   32.____

    A. plastering   B. papering   C. roofing   D. bricklaying

33. In plastering, coves would *most likely* be found where   33.____

    A. wall meets ceiling   B. one wall meets another
    C. wall meets floor   D. wall meets column

34. Fire stopping is usually accomplished by   34.____

    A. installing self-closing doors
    B. bricking up the space between furring at floors
    C. installing wire glass
    D. using fire resistive materials throughout the building

35. A Class 1 (fireproof structure) building has floor sleepers of wood. This is   35.____

    A. *not permitted*
    B. *permitted*
    C. *permitted* if the space between sleepers is filled with incombustible material
    D. *permitted* if a wearing surface similar to asphalt tile is applied to the wooden flooring

KEY (CORRECT ANSWERS)

1.	A		16.	B
2.	B		17.	D
3.	C		18.	A
4.	A		19.	D
5.	C		20.	C
6.	B		21.	B
7.	D		22.	C
8.	B		23.	A
9.	C		24.	C
10.	A		25.	B
11.	A		26.	D
12.	C		27.	A
13.	D		28.	B
14.	C		29.	D
15.	A		30.	B

31. A
32. D
33. A
34. B
35. C

_____

TEST 2

DIRECTIONS: Each question or incomplete statement is followed by several suggested answers or completions. Select the one that BEST answers the question or completes the statement. *PRINT THE LETTER OF THE CORRECT ANSWER IN THE SPACE AT THE RIGHT.*

1. Joints on interior surfaces of brick walls are usually flush joints EXCEPT when the walls are to be   1.____

    A. painted   B. plastered
    C. waterproofed   D. dampproofed

2. The headers in a brick veneer wall serve   2.____

    A. both a structural and an architectural purpose
    B. a structural purpose only
    C. an architectural purpose only
    D. NO structural or architectural purpose

3. Of the following, the one which is NOT usually classified as interior wood trim is   3.____

    A. apron   B. ribbon   C. jamb   D. base mold

4. Single-strength glass would *most likely* be found in   4.____

    A. single light sash
    B. doors in fire walls
    C. doors in fire partitions
    D. multi-light sash

5. The one of the following items that is LEAST related to the others is   5.____

    A. newel   B. riser   C. nosing   D. sill

6. In a plastered room, grounds for plaster are LEAST likely to be used   6.____

    A. at baseboards   B. around windows
    C. around doors   D. at the top of wainscoting

7. Of the following types of walls, the type which is *most likely* an interior wall is _____ wall.   7.____

    A. curtain   B. faced   C. panel   D. fire

8. *Boxing* is *most likely* to be performed by a   8.____

    A. mason   B. plasterer
    C. plumber   D. painter

9. Linseed oil is classified as a   9.____

    A. vehicle   B. thinner
    C. drying oil   D. pigment

10. Curing of concrete would be MOST critical when the temperature and humidity are, respectively,   10.____

    A. 75° and 80%   B. 80° and 90%
    C. 85° and 10%   D. 90° and 95%

11. Of the following items, the item which is LEAST related to the others is   11.____

    A. putty   B. sash weight
    C. glazier's points   D. lights

12. Assume that a wood-frame house has studs of 2 x 4's.   12.____
Placing the studs so that the wider dimension is parallel to the wall is

    A. *good* because it provides a wider nailing surface for sheathing and lathing
    B. *bad* because it reduces the open space available for windows
    C. *good* because it stiffens the frame
    D. *bad* because it reduces the load-carrying capacity of the studs

13. Government anchors are used in one of the following types of construction. Which one?   13.____

    A. Wood frame
    B. Steel beams supported on masonry bearing walls
    C. Wooden joists on masonry bearing walls
    D. Steel frame with steel joists

14. When rivet holes in structural steel fail to match up by an eighth of an inch, the BEST thing to do is   14.____

    A. ignore the mismatch and force the rivet into the hole
    B. enlarge the holes with a drift pin
    C. ream the holes to a larger diameter
    D. use a smaller sized rivet

15. The BEST way to use two angles to make a lintel is   15.____

    A.   B.   C.   D.

16. A single channel section would *most likely* be used for a   16.____

    A. floor beam   B. girder
    C. spandrel beam   D. column

17. An oil-base paint is usually thinned with   17.____

    A. linseed oil   B. turpentine
    C. a drying oil   D. a resin

18. Red lead is often used as a pigment in metal priming paints PRIMARILY because it   18.____

    A. provides good coverage   B. presents a good appearance
    C. makes painting easier   D. is a rust inhibitor

19. Knots in wood that is to be painted 19._____

   A. require no special treatment
   B. should be painted with the priming paint before the priming paint is applied to the rest of the wood
   C. should be coated with linseed oil before any painting is done
   D. should be coated with shellac before any painting is done

20. A dove-tail anchor would *most likely* be used to bond brick veneer with a _____ wall. 20._____

   A. brick   B. concrete   C. wood frame   D. concrete block

21. A rafter is MOST similar in function to a 21._____

   A. joist   B. stud   C. sill   D. girder

22. In steel construction, it is usually MOST important to mill the ends of 22._____

   A. beams   B. girders   C. columns   D. lintels

23. Furring tile is usually set so that the air spaces in the tile are 23._____

   A. continuous in a vertical direction
   B. continuous in a horizontal direction
   C. closed off at the ends of each tile
   D. set at random

24. When plastering a wall surface of glazed tile, it is MOST important that the tile 24._____

   A. be wet   B. be dry
   C. be scored   D. joints be raked

25. In a peaked roof, the run of a rafter is 25._____

   A. less than the length of the rafter
   B. greater than the length of the rafter
   C. equal to the length of the rafter
   D. dependent upon the slope of the rafter

26. Construction of a dormer window does NOT usually involve 26._____

   A. cut rafters   B. rafter headers
   C. trimmer rafters   D. hip rafters

27. In a four-ply slag roof, 27._____

   A. there is no overlap of the roofing felt
   B. a uniform coating of pitch or asphalt is placed on top of the top layer of felt
   C. slag is placed between the layers of felt
   D. there is no need to use flashing

28. Copper wire basket strainers would *most likely* be used by a 28._____

   A. carpenter   B. plumber   C. painter   D. roofer

29. Splices of columns in steel construction are usually made   29.____

    A. at floor level
    B. two feet above floor level
    C. two feet below floor level
    D. midway between floors

30. In plumbing, a lead bend is usually used in the line from a   30.____

    A. slop sink   B. shower
    C. water closet   D. kitchen sink

31. The location of leaks in gas piping may be BEST detected by use of a   31.____

    A. match   B. heated filament
    C. soapy water solution   D. guinea pig

32. The one of the following items that would be MOST useful in eliminating water hammer   32.____
from a water system is a

    A. magnesium anode   B. surge tank
    C. clean out   D. quick-closing valve

33. The MAIN purpose of a fixture trap is to   33.____

    A. catch small articles that may have accidentally dropped in the fixture
    B. prevent back syphonage
    C. make it easier to repair the fixture
    D. block the passage of foul air

34. In a certain district, the area of a building may be no longer than 55% of the area of the   34.____
lot on which it stands. On a rectangular lot 75 ft. by 125 ft., the maximum permissible
area of building is, in square feet, *most nearly*

    A. 5148   B. 5152   C. 5156   D. 5160

35. The allowable tensile stress in steel is 18,000 pounds per square inch. The maximum   35.____
permissible tensile load in a 1-inch diameter steel bar is, in pounds, *most nearly*

    A. 13,500   B. 13,800   C. 14,100   D. 14,400

————

KEY (CORRECT ANSWERS)

1.	B		16.	C
2.	C		17.	B
3.	B		18.	D
4.	D		19.	D
5.	D		20.	B
6.	D		21.	A
7.	D		22.	C
8.	D		23.	B
9.	A		24.	C
10.	C		25.	A
11.	B		26.	D
12.	B		27.	B
13.	B		28.	D
14.	C		29.	B
15.	A		30.	C

31.	C
32.	B
33.	D
34.	C
35.	C

TEST 3

DIRECTIONS: Each question or incomplete statement is followed by several suggested answers or completions. Select the one that BEST answers the question or completes the statement. *PRINT THE LETTER OF THE CORRECT ANSWER IN THE SPACE AT THE RIGHT.*

1. The ends of a joist in a brick building are cut to a bevel. This is done PRINCIPALLY to prevent damage to

   A. joist   B. floor   C. sill   D. wall

1.____

2. Of the following, the wood that is MOST commonly used today for floor joists is

   A. long leaf yellow pine   B. douglas fir
   C. oak   D. birch

2.____

3. Quarter sawed lumber is preferred for the best finished flooring PRINCIPALLY because it

   A. has the greatest strength
   B. shrinks the least
   C. is the easiest to nail
   D. is the easiest to handle

3.____

4. Of the following, the MAXIMUM height that would be considered acceptable for a stair riser is

   A. 6 1/2"   B. 7 1/2"   C. 8 1/2"   D. 9 1/2"

4.____

5. The part of a tree that will produce the DENSEST wood is the _____ wood.

   A. spring   B. summer   C. sap   D. heart

5.____

6. Lumber in quantity is ordered by

   A. cubic feet   B. foot board measure
   C. lineal feet   D. weight and length

6.____

7. A *chase* in a brick wall is a

   A. pilaster   B. waterstop   C. recess   D. corbel

7.____

8. *Parging* refers to

   A. increasing the thickness of a brick wall
   B. plastering the back of face brickwork
   C. bonding face brick to backing blocks
   D. leveling each course of brick

8.____

9. In brickwork, muriatic acid is commonly used to

   A. increase the strength of the mortar
   B. etch the brick
   C. waterproof the wall
   D. clean the wall

9.____

10. Cement mortar can be made easier to work by the addition of a small quantity of   10.____

    A. lime   B. soda   C. litharge   D. plaster

11. Joints in brick walls are tooled   11.____

    A. immediately after each brick is laid
    B. after the mortar has had its initial set
    C. after the entire wall is completed
    D. 28 days after the wall has been built

12. If cement mortar has begun to set before it can be used in a wall, the BEST thing to do is to   12.____

    A. use the mortar immediately as is
    B. add a small quantity of lime
    C. add some water and mix thoroughly
    D. discard the mortar

13. The BEST flux to use when soldering galvanized iron is   13.____

    A. killed acid   B. sal-ammoniac
    C. muriatic acid   D. resin

14. The type of solder that would be used in *hard soldering* is _____ solder.   14.____

    A. bismuth   B. wiping   C. 50-50   D. silver

15. Roll roofing material is usually felt which has been impregnated with   15.____

    A. cement   B. mastic   C. tar   D. latex

16. The purpose of flashing on roofs is to   16.____

    A. secure roofing materials to the roof
    B. make it easier to lay the roofing
    C. prevent leaks through the roof
    D. insulate the roof from excessive heat

17. The type of chain used with sash weights is _____ link.   17.____

    A. flat   B. round
    C. figure-eight   D. basketweave

18. The material that would be used to seal around a window frame is   18.____

    A. oakum   B. litharge   C. grout   D. calking

19. The function of a window sill is *most nearly* the same as that of a   19.____

    A. jamb   B. coping   C. lintel   D. buck

20. Lightweight plaster would be made with   20.____

    A. sand   B. cinders   C. potash   D. vermiculite

21. The FIRST coat of plaster to be applied on a three-coat plaster job is the _____ coat.   21.____

    A. brown   B. scratch   C. white   D. keene

22. The FIRST coat of plaster over rock lath should be a _____ plaster.

    A. gypsum   B. lime
    C. Portland cement   D. pozzolan cement

22.____

23. The PRINCIPAL reason for covering a concrete sidewalk with straw or paper after the concrete has been poured is to

    A. prevent people from walking on the concrete while it is still wet
    B. impart a rough, non-slip surface to the concrete
    C. prevent excessive evaporation of water in the concrete
    D. shorten the length of time it would take for the concrete to harden

23.____

24. Concrete is *rubbed* with a(n)

    A. emery wheel   B. carborundum brick
    C. sandstone   D. alundum stick

24.____

25. To prevent concrete from sticking to forms, the forms should be painted with

    A. oil   B. kerosene   C. water   D. lime

25.____

26. One method of measuring the consistency of a concrete mix is by means of a _____ test.

    A. penetration   B. flow
    C. slump   D. weight

26.____

27. A chemical that is sometimes used to prevent the freezing of concrete in cold weather is

    A. alum   B. glycerine
    C. calcium chloride   D. sodium nitrate

27.____

28. The one of the following that is LEAST commonly used for columns is

    A. wide flange beams   B. angles
    C. concrete-filled pipe   D. "I" beams

28.____

29. Fire protection of steel floor beams is MOST frequently accomplished by the use of

    A. gypsum block   B. brick
    C. rock wool fill   D. vermiculite gypsum plaster

29.____

30. A *Pittsburgh look* is a(n)

    A. emergency door lock   B. sheet metal joint
    C. elevator safety   D. boiler valve

30.____

31. Of the following items, the one which is NOT used in making fastenings to masonry or plaster walls is a(n)

    A. lead shield   B. expansion bolt
    C. rawl plug   D. steel bushing

31.____

32. The term *bell and spigot* USUALLY refers to

    A. refrigerator motors   B. cast iron pipes
    C. steam radiator outlets   D. electrical receptacles

32.____

33. In plumbing work, a valve which allows water to flow in one direction only is commonly known as a _____ valve.

33.____

    A. check   B. globe   C. gate   D. stop

34. A pipe coupling is BEST used to connect two pieces of pipe of

34.____

    A. the same diameter in a straight line
    B. the same diameter at right angles to each other
    C. different diameters at a 45° angle
    D. different diameters in a 1/8th bend

35. One method of testing fuses is to connect a pair of test lamps in the circuit in such a manner that the test lamp will light up if the fuse is good and will remain dark if the fuse is bad. In the illustration, 1 and 2 are fuses. In order to test if fuse 1 is bad, test lamps should be connected between

35.____

    A. A and B   B. B and D   C. A and D   D. C and B

36. Operating an incandescent electric light bulb at less than its rated voltage will result in

36.____

    A. shorter life and brighter light
    B. longer life and dimmer light
    C. brighter light and longer life
    D. dimmer light and shorter life

37. In order to control a lamp from two different positions, it is necessary to use

37.____

    A. two single pole switches
    B. one single pole switch and one four-way switch
    C. two three-way switches
    D. one single pole switch and one four-way switch

38. The PRINCIPAL reason for the grounding of electrical equipment and circuits is to

38.____

    A. prevent short circuits   B. insure safety from shock
    C. save power   D. increase voltage

39. The ordinary single-pole flush wall type switch must be connected

39.____

    A. across the line
    B. in the "hot" conductor
    C. in the grounded conductor
    D. in the white conductor

40. A strike plate is MOST closely associated with a

40.____

    A. lock   B. sash   C. butt   D. tie rod

41. A room is 7'6" wide by 9'0" long, with a ceiling height of 8'0". One gallon of flat paint will cover approximately 400 square feet of wall.
The number of gallons of this paint required to paint the walls of this room, making no deductions for windows or doors, is *most nearly* _____ gallon.

    A. 1/4   B. 1/3   C. 3/4   D. 1

41.____

42. The cost of a certain job is broken down as follows:

    Materials $375
    Rental of equipment   120
    Labor   315

The percentage of the total cost of the job that can be charged to materials is *most nearly*

    A. 40%   B. 42%   C. 44%   D. 46%

42.____

43. By trial, it is found that by using two cubic feet of sand, a 5 cubic foot batch of concrete is produced. Using the same proportions, the amount of sand required to produce 2 cubic yards of concrete is *most nearly* _____ cubic feet.

    A. 20   B. 22   C. 24   D. 26

43.____

44. It takes four men six days to do a certain job. Working at the same speed, the number of days it will take three men to do this job is

    A. 7   B. 8   C. 9   D. 10

44.____

45. The cost of rawl plugs is $2.75 per gross. The cost of 2,448 rawl plugs is

    A. $46.75   B. $47.25   C. $47.75   D. $48.25

45.____

KEY (CORRECT ANSWERS)

1. D	11. B	21. B	31. D	41. C
2. B	12. D	22. A	32. B	42. D
3. B	13. C	23. C	33. A	43. B
4. B	14. D	24. B	34. A	44. B
5. D	15. C	25. A	35. C	45. A
6. B	16. C	26. C	36. B	
7. C	17. A	27. C	37. C	
8. B	18. D	28. B	38. B	
9. D	19. B	29. D	39. B	
10. A	20. D	30. B	40. A	

EXAMINATION SECTION
TEST 1

DIRECTIONS: Each question or incomplete statement is followed by several suggested answers or completions. Select the one that BEST answers the question or completes the statement. *PRINT THE LETTER OF THE CORRECT ANSWER IN THE SPACE AT THE RIGHT.*

1. The sketch below shows a concrete building wall and footing with a dumbbell shaped sheet of rubber joining then.

1._____

The MAIN purpose of the sheet of rubber between the footing and the wall is to

    A. cut down the loss of heat from the building
    B. prevent termites from entering into the building through the joint
    C. prevent the flow of water through the joint
    D. provide a flexible joint between the wall and the footing

2. A chase is USUALLY put on the inside face of a brick wall to

2._____

    A. allow for expansion of the wall
    B. provide space for a pipe
    C. act as a mortar drop during construction
    D. moisture-proof the back side of the wall

3. The sketch below shows a cap stone set on a brick wall.

3._____

The MAIN purpose of the groove marked X in the cap stone is to

    A. save on material
    B. make the projection appear smaller
    C. prevent rainwater on the cap stone from reaching the wall
    D. provide a finger grip when setting the cap stone

4. The sketch shown below represents a part of a brick wall.

4.____

The type of mortar joint shown in the diagram is known as a _____ joint.

A. weathered   B. raked   C. cut   D. struck

Questions 5-8.

DIRECTIONS: Questions 5 through 8 refer to the FRONT ELEVATION OF A BRICK BUILD-ING shown below.

5. The brick indicated by letter V is called a

5.____

  A. header   B. rowlock   C. corbel   D. stretcher

6. The cap stone W is known as a

6.____

  A. baffling   B. plinthing
  C. creneling   D. coping

7. The reinforced concrete beam X is a

7.____

  A. lintel   B. batten   C. stile   D. rafter

8. The part of the wall Y that extends above the roof is the

8.____

  A. parapet   B. wainscot   C. apron   D. skirt

9. The term *corbelling* generally refers to

9.____

  A. the cutting of flagstones with a circular saw to form circular pieces
  B. the erection of a scaffold to lay a circular brick wall

C. a method of constructing concrete walls by pouring the concrete in flat panels and then tilting them into a vertical position

D. the stepping out of several courses of brick to form a ledge

10. In masonry cavity or veneer walls, the PURPOSE of providing an opening through the mortar joints at regular intervals is to allow for

10.____

A. lateral expansion
B. drainage of moisture
C. inspection of the brick work
D. the insertion of expansion bolts

11. The sketch below shows a reinforced concrete wall and footing.

11.____

The concrete section marked E is USUALLY called a

A. balustrade
B. buttress
C. breach
D. branch

12. The sketch shown at the right is the plan of a concrete column. The bevel X on each corner is known as a(n)

12.____

A. kerf
B. incline
C. chamfer
D. bend

13. The process of keeping freshly poured concrete damp for a period of days after it is poured is known as

13.____

A. curing
B. hibernating
C. dousing
D. bathing

14. Concrete, mixed at a central plant and ready to be poured at time of delivery at a job site, is known as _____ concrete.

14.____

A. haul-mix
B. ready-mix
C. house-mix
D. precast

15. The test on fresh concrete to show its stiffness is known as the _____ test.

15.____

A. slump
B. slop
C. slack
D. slip

16. A brick masonry wall is leaking because the mortar joints have cracked.   16.____
The process of cutting away the defective mortar to a depth of at least 1/2 inch and
then replacing it with the proper mortar is called _____ pointing.

    A. score   B. jack   C. channel   D. tuck

17. The grooved wheels in a block used in raising loads are known as   17.____

    A. pins   B. shackles   C. beckets   D. sheaves

18. Of the following devices, the one that should be used for raising and lowering heavy   18.____
stones is a(n)

    A. windlass   B. adze   C. cant   D. jitney

19. A spall is a _____ brick.   19.____

    A. blistered   B. chip of a
    C. pockmarked   D. scored

20. A snap tie would be used MOST often in the construction of a _____ wall.   20.____

    A. brick   B. concrete block
    C. concrete   D. rubble

KEY (CORRECT ANSWERS)

1.	C		11.	B
2.	B		12.	C
3.	C		13.	A
4.	B		14.	B
5.	A		15.	A
6.	D		16.	D
7.	A		17.	D
8.	A		18.	A
9.	D		19.	B
10.	B		20.	C

TEST 2

DIRECTIONS: Each question or incomplete statement is followed by several suggested answers or completions. Select the one that BEST answers the question or completes the statement. *PRINT THE LETTER OF THE CORRECT ANSWER IN THE SPACE AT THE RIGHT.*

1. The MAIN reason for oiling the inside faces of wood forms against which concrete will be placed is to   1.____

    A.   prevent the formation of hairline cracks in the concrete
    B.   give the concrete surface a darker color tone
    C.   prevent the forms from sticking to the concrete
    D.   accelerate the setting of the concrete

2. After placing fresh concrete in the wood forms of a floor slab, water containing fine parti-   2.____
    cles may rise to the surface.
    This will occur MOST frequently if the

    A.   concrete is vibrated excessively
    B.   concrete is dropped into the form from a wheelbarrow
    C.   aggregate is very dry
    D.   temperature of the fresh concrete rises to 90°F

3. Thin, dressed, squared stone used for facing a wall is known as   3.____

    A.   ashlar   B.   strap   C.   fillet   D.   mill

4. A special type of portland cement which causes the concrete to harden more quickly   4.____
    than ordinary portland cement is USUALLY known as _____ cement.

    A.   fast-hardening   B.   high-early-strength
    C.   air-entrained   D.   extra-ordinary

5. In cavity wall construction, the metal wires placed between the two separate parts of the   5.____
    wall are known as

    A.   stirrups   B.   escutcheons
    C.   ties   D.   girts

6. The type of scaffold that is MOST frequently used when repointing leaky brick joints near   6.____
    the top of a high-rise brick apartment building that has no fire escapes is the _____
    scaffold.

    A.   trestle   B.   swing
    C.   wood pole   D.   rolling

7. Of the following items, the ones that should be used to fasten wood strips to a masonry   7.____
    wall are masonry

    A.   wedges   B.   splints   C.   nails   D.   spiders

8. Of the following types of brick, the one that should be used to line the inside surface of a   8.____
    boiler furnace is the _____ brick.

    A.   face   B.   glazed   C.   fire   D.   enameled

9. A strong water-proof material that is used to cover equipment to protect it from rain or snow is a

    A. template   B. trammel
    C. trabeate   D. tarpaulin

9._____

10. The bottom of a reinforced concrete column USUALLY rests on a

    A. bed   B. footing   C. grillage   D. plate

10._____

11. A hand cutting tool that resembles a small pick and is used by bricklayers for fire brick work is known as a(n)

    A. adze   B. gaff   C. scutch   D. chip

11._____

12. Of the following, the building member that is LEAST related to the others in function is the

    A. pier   B. column   C. pilaster   D. sill

12._____

13. A course of 4" x 2 3/8" x 8" bricks is set in a wall so that the 2 3/8" x 8" side is in the front face of the wall with the 8" length vertical.
This course is called a _____ course.

    A. rowlock   B. soldier   C. king   D. belt

13._____

14. A kiln should LEAST likely be used to

    A. dry lumber   B. burn lime
    C. bake brick   D. dry concrete

14._____

15. In the construction of a brick wall, the LAST brick which finishes a horizontal course is known as the _____ brick.

    A. clincher   B. closer   C. liner   D. keyer

15._____

16. Of the following locations, a concrete culvert would MOST likely be found

    A. on a roof of a building   B. under a roadway
    C. under a tunnel   D. on a wharf

16._____

17. Of the following, the MOST practical device to use to deposit fresh concrete in places that are difficult to reach is a

    A. scupper   B. scuttle   C. catamaran   D. chute

17._____

18. Of the following types of rope, the one that is MOST susceptible to dry rot when not stored properly is

    A. nylon   B. manila
    C. polyester   D. polypropylene

18._____

19. Of the following locations, an outrigger should MOST often be built

    A. on a roof   B. in a basement
    C. in a dumbwaiter   D. in a boiler furnace

19._____

20. A mixture of hydrochloric acid (1 part by volume) and water (4 parts by volume) used to   20.____
remove mortar stains from brick is known as _____ acid.

   A. builder's   B. mason's   C. Dutch   D. French

———

KEY (CORRECT ANSWERS)

1.	C	11.	C
2.	A	12.	D
3.	A	13.	B
4.	B	14.	D
5.	C	15.	B
6.	B	16.	B
7.	C	17.	D
8.	C	18.	B
9.	D	19.	A
10.	B	20.	A

———

TEST 3

DIRECTIONS: Each question or incomplete statement is followed by several suggested answers or completions. Select the one that BEST answers the question or completes the statement. *PRINT THE LETTER OF THE CORRECT ANSWER IN THE SPACE AT THE RIGHT.*

1. A pure cement uncut by a sand mixture is known as _____ cement.   1._____

    A. unspiked   B. mason's   C. white   D. neat

2. In reinforced concrete work, the diameter of a #6 reinforcing bar is MOST NEARLY   2._____
    _____ inch.

    A. 1/4   B. 1/2   C. 5/8   D. 3/4

3. In a 1:2: 3 1/4 concrete sidewalk mix, the 3 1/4 refers to the   3._____

    A. cement   B. admixture   C. stone   D. sand

4. Cinder concrete block is SUPERIOR to stone concrete block in   4._____

    A. strength   B. the ability to insulate
    C. durability   D. appearance

5. The sketch shown at the right shows the top of a concrete   5._____
    block.
    The block is called a
    A. broach
    B. bull nose
    C. buffer
    D. bollard

6. Lampblack is used in concrete for sidewalks PRIMARILY to   6._____

    A. make the concrete surface slip-proof
    B. give the concrete a darker shade
    C. accelerate the setting of the concrete
    D. increase the strength of the concrete

7. *Honeycomb* is a defect that occurs in   7._____

    A. concrete   B. plaster
    C. common brick   D. glass brick

8. Common red brick is composed PRIMARILY of   8._____

    A. clay   B. sand
    C. asbestos   D. hydrated lime

9. The substance, which when added to a concrete mix gives it color, is known as a   9._____

    A. vehicle   B. solvent   C. charger   D. pigment

10. Of the following materials, the one that is used as an aggregate in lightweight concrete is   10._____

    A. transite   B. hematite   C. bauxite   D. perlite

11. The weight of a cubic foot of concrete, made of regular cement, sand, and stone, is MOST NEARLY _____ lbs.   11.____

    A. 100   B. 125   C. 150   D. 175

12. Of the following materials, the one that is USUALLY used to fill the expansion joint of a reinforced concrete roadway slab poured on earth is a premolded _____ filler.   12.____

    A. gypsum   B. mastic   C. plaster   D. lead

13. In first class reinforced concrete work, the horizontal reinforcement in a floor slab is USUALLY supported on   13.____

    A. bollards   B. bolsters   C. battens   D. bats

14. A masonry block provided with a groove to receive metal flashing is known as a _____ block.   14.____

    A. raggle or reglet   B. random or irregular
    C. ranger or soldier   D. ratchet or slope

15. The 3/4" space between the bottom of a pump bed plate and the top of the concrete foundation supporting it should USUALLY be filled with   15.____

    A. plaster of paris   B. a caulking compound
    C. a grout mixture   D. bitumastic asphalt

16. In a concrete mix of 1:2:2 3/4, the 1 refers to the amount of   16.____

    A. admixture   B. coarse aggregate
    C. sand   D. cement

17. In a 1:1:6 mortar mix, the 6 refers to the amount of   17.____

    A. sand   B. lime
    C. coarse aggregate   D. cement

18. The number of bags of cement in 3/4 of a barrel of cement is MOST NEARLY   18.____

    A. 2   B. 2 1/2   C. 3   D. 3 3/4

19. In building construction, pieces of material which have been rejected as not suitable to be used are known as   19.____

    A. curds   B. culls   C. cairns   D. cusps

20. The sketch shown at the right shows the top of a concrete block.
Of the following locations, this block should MOST often be used   20.____

KEY (CORRECT ANSWERS)

1.	D	11.	C
2.	D	12.	B
3.	C	13.	B
4.	B	14.	A
5.	B	15.	C
6.	B	16.	D
7.	A	17.	A
8.	A	18.	C
9.	D	19.	B
10.	D	20.	A

———

TEST 4

DIRECTIONS: Each question or incomplete statement is followed by several suggested answers or completions. Select the one that BEST answers the question or completes the statement. *PRINT THE LETTER OF THE CORRECT ANSWER IN THE SPACE AT THE RIGHT.*

1. Of the following, the tool MOST frequently used by a bricklayer is a   1.____

   A. trowel   B. jointer   C. hoe   D. shovel

2. Fresh concrete is usually poured under water by using vertical steel pipe and a hopper   2.____
   for receiving the concrete.
   This method is known as the _____ method.

   A. Frasch   B. Proctor   C. Tremie   D. Atterberg

3. The shape of the face of the head of a bricklayer's hammer is   3.____

   A. round   B. square
   C. elliptical   D. hexagonal

4. The metal or wood tool used to strike off and level freshly poured concrete is a   4.____

   A. screed   B. squeegee   C. slicker   D. scupper

5.   5.____

The tool shown in the above sketch is a concrete

   A. placer   B. kumalong   C. flute   D. rake

6. The tool shown in the sketch at the right is a   6.____

   A. bricklayer's set
   B. wire lather's cutter
   C. stone mason's chisel
   D. concrete mason's caulker 8"

7. Of the following, the heater that is MOST frequently used in the winter time to heat the air   7.____
   around freshly poured concrete to prevent the concrete from freezing is a

   A. Davy lamp   B. Bunsen burner
   C. salamander   D. skewer

8. The tool shown in the sketch at the right is a _____ trowel.   8.____
   A. buttering
   B. cross joint
   C. gauging
   D. duck bill

   1 3/4" HEEL

   4 3/4"

9. Shown at the right is a sketch of a knot used in rigging. The knot is a _____ hitch.   9.____

   A. timber
   B. timber hitch and a half
   C. half
   D. clove

   TIMBER

10. For maximum safety when using an 18-foot ladder set against a wall, the helper should place the base of the ladder so that it extends from the face of the wall a distance of MOST NEARLY   10.____

    A. 2'6"   B. 4'6"   C. 6'0"   D. 9'0"

11. Of the following types of fire extinguisher, the BEST one to use on a gasoline fire is   11.____

    A. soda acid   B. pump tank
    C. foam   D. cartridge actuated

12. The handles of a loaded wheelbarrow should be raised to the traveling position by lifting with the   12.____

    A. back muscles, keeping the back stooped backwards from the vertical position
    B. back muscles, keeping the back stooped forward from the vertical position
    C. leg muscles, keeping the back in a vertical position
    D. leg muscles, keeping the back in a horizontal position

13. The number of cubic feet in a concrete sidewalk consisting of fifteen squares 5 feet by 5 feet by 4 inches deep is MOST NEARLY   13.____

    A. 100   B. 125   C. 250   D. 600

14. The sketch at the right shows a section of a concrete wall.
    The dimension X has a value of MOST NEARLY   14.____

    A. 2' 7,3/4"
    B. 2' 8 1/4"
    C. 2' 9 1/2"
    D. 2' 10 3/4"

    2'6"

    1
    12

    4'9"

    X

15. The total number of cubic feet of concrete in twenty-three round concrete fence post foot-   15.____
    ings, the dimension of which are 3 feet by 8 inches in diameter (neglect the volume of the
    pipe), is MOST NEARLY

    A. 19   B. 21   C. 23   D. 25

16. The run of a reinforced concrete staircase which has 11 steps, each 9 1/2 inches wide   16.____
    (exclusive of the nosing), is

    A. 7'11"   B. 8'9"   C. 9'6"   D. 10'2"

Questions 17-19.

DIRECTIONS: Questions 17 through 19 are to be answered SOLELY on the basis of the fol-
               lowing passage.

*It is best to avoid surface water on freshly poured concrete in the first place. However,
when there is a very small amount present, the recommended procedure is to allow it to evapo-
rate before finishing. If there is considerable water, it is removed with a broom, belt, float, or by
other convenient means. It is never good practice to sprinkle dry cement, or a mixture of
cement and fine aggregate, on concrete to take up surface water. Such fine materials form a
layer on the surface that is likely to dust or hair check when the concrete hardens.*

17. The MAIN subject of the above passage is: 17.____

    A. Surface cracking of concrete
    B. Evaporation of water from freshly poured concrete
    C. Removing surface water from concrete
    D. Final adjustments of ingredients in the concrete mix

18. According to the passage, the sprinkling of dry cement on the surface of a concrete mix   18.____
    would MOST likely

    A. prevent the mix from setting
    B. cause discoloration on the surface of the concrete
    C. cause the coarse aggregate to settle out too quickly
    D. cause powdering and small cracks on the surface of the concrete

19. According to the passage, the thing to do when considerable surface water is present on   19.____
    the freshly poured concrete is to

    A. dump the concrete back into the mixer and drain the water
    B. allow the water to evaporate before finishing
    C. remove the water with a broom, belt, or float
    D. add more fine aggregate but not cement

20. Scaffolds shall be level and set on *firm* ground.   20.____
    As used in the above sentence, the word *firm* means MOST NEARLY

    A. stable   B. loose   C. weak   D. flimsy

KEY (CORRECT ANSWERS)

1. A	11. C
2. C	12. C
3. B	13. B
4. A	14. D
5. D	15. C
6. C	16. B
7. C	17. C
8. B	18. D
9. C	19. C
10. B	20. A

EXAMINATION SECTION
TEST 1

DIRECTIONS: Each question or incomplete statement is followed by several suggested
answers or completions. Select the one that BEST answers the question or
completes the statement. *PRINT THE LETTER OF THE CORRECT ANSWER
IN THE SPACE AT THE RIGHT.*

1. In a building, furring is USUALLY attached to the inside of a brick wall by galvanized   1.____

    A. pins   B. screws
    C. ties   D. anchor bolts

2. Brick is sometimes dipped in water before laying because   2.____

    A. the bricklayer prefers to handle wet brick
    B. the moisture absorbed makes the brick heavier
    C. a wet brick will not take moisture from the mortar
    D. a wet brick will not break as easily as a dry one

3. A piece of lumber measures 6 inches wide by 2 inches thick by 8 feet long. The number   3.____
of board feet contained in the piece is

    A. 8   B. 10   C. 12   D. 48

4. The sum of 1/12 and 1/4 is   4.____

    A. 1/3   B. 5/12   C. 7/12   D. 3/8

5. The product of 12 and 2 1/3 is   5.____

    A. 27   B. 28   C. 29   D. 30

6. If 4 1/2 is subtracted from 7 1/5, the remainder is   6.____

    A. 3 7/10   B. 2 7/10   C. 3 3/10   D. 2 3/10

7. A slump test is performed on   7.____

    A. brick   B. wood   C. steel   D. concrete

8. In brick work, a course consisting of bricks set upon their sides is known as a _____   8.____
course.

    A. soldier   B. rowlock   C. header   D. stretcher

9. A small vertical recess or hollowed-out portion of a brick wall is called a   9.____
    A. chase   B. gable   C. corbel   D. cope

10. Mortar for brick work MOST usually consists of   10.____

    A. lime, cement, and sand
    B. cement, sand, and water
    C. lime, cement, and water
    D. lime, cement, sand, and water

11. If mortar acquires an initial set (that is, becomes too stiff to work), it should be 11._____

    A. remixed without adding water
    B. remixed with added water
    C. used as it is
    D. discarded

12. A header brick differs from a stretcher brick in 12._____

    A. size   B. shape
    C. surface finish   D. position in the wall

13. The expression *two by four* refers to 13._____

    A. mortar   B. stone   C. wood   D. brick

14. Cut stone used in the construction of a brick wall would NOT be used for 14._____

    A. sills   B. coping   C. trip   D. backing

15. The length, thickness, and width of common brick are, in inches, respectively, 15._____

    A. 8 x 2 x 4   B. 6 x 2 1/4 x 3 3/4
    C. 8 x 6 x 3 3/4   D. 8 x 2 1/4 x 33

16. The terms *raked, struck, weather* are MOST likely to be used in the construction of 16._____

    A. walls   B. roofs   C. floors   D. foundations

17. The furrow in the mortar of a bed joint should be 17._____

    A. deep
    B. shallow
    C. wide
    D. parallel to the short side of the brick

18. Before starting to lay the bricks, mortar for bed joints should be spread out over a number of bricks. In general practice, this number is MOST NEARLY 18._____

    A. 32   B. 16   C. 8   D. 4

19. Of the following methods of making head joints in stretcher courses, the POOREST one is 19._____

    A. put plenty of mortar on the end of the brick and shove it into place
    B. spot a dab of mortar on the brick already in place, then throw plenty of mortar on it, and finally shove the brick being laid into this mortar
    C. shove the brick into a deep bed of mortar
    D. place the brick without mortar and then slush the joint

20. An inspector removes a brick which has just been laid. If the mortar does not adhere to the brick, it is an indication that 20._____

    A. the joint was not properly furrowed
    B. something is wrong with the mortar
    C. too much mortar was used
    D. not enough mortar was used

21. In masonry work, spalls are   21.____

    A. stones which have been rejected
    B. small stones used for closures
    C. chips of stone
    D. key-shaped bricks

22. Centering is used by a(n)   22.____

    A. electrician   B. bricklayer
    C. plumber   D. plasterer

23. A lintel is used in a   23.____

    A. roof   B. wall   C. floor   D. footing

24. Tooling of face joints in brick work should be done   24.____

    A. immediately after the brick is laid
    B. after the mortar has acquired initial set
    C. after the mortar has acquired final set
    D. on extensive jobs, after the wall is completed

25. A wall consists of stone facing and brick backing. Parging (or pargeting) should be done   25.____
with

    A. stone-setting mortar
    B. brick mortar
    C. either type of mortar
    D. a mortar other than the two types specified

26. A worker's hourly rate is $8.52. If he works 11 1/2 hours, he should receive   26.____

    A. $97.38   B. $97.98   C. $ 98.61   D. $99.18

27. Water freezes at _____°F.   27.____

    A. 0   B. 100   C. 50   D. 32

28. In brick work, pointing means   28.____

    A. laying brick at an angle
    B. filling exposed joints with mortar
    C. using the point of the trowel to furrow a bed
    D. laying the brick to a particular pattern

29. A dove-tail anchor would MOST likely be used to anchor   29.____

    A. individual bricks to one another
    B. individual stones to one another
    C. facing brick to terra cotta backing
    D. masonry facing to a concrete wall

30. A bonding or brushing mortar with a consistency of cream would MOST probably be used to lay

    A.   common brick   B.   face brick
    C.   cinder concrete block   D.   insulating fire brick

30.____

31. Upon opening a bag of cement, you find that there are many lumps in it which you cannot crumble in your hand. The BEST thing to do is to

    A.   remove the lumps before using the cement
    B.   discard the entire bag
    C.   break up the lumps with a hammer
    D.   use the cement as is

31.____

32. Twenty pints of water just fill a pail. The capacity of the pail, in gallons, is

    A. 2   B. 2 1/4   C. 2 1/2   D. 2 3/4

32.____

33. It is good practice to have the bottom of a footing for a wall at least four feet below the surface of the ground. This depth is specified to

    A.   insure that the earth will provide a good support for the footing
    B.   keep the bottom of the footing below the frost line
    C.   allow for a shallow cellar
    D.   keep the footing from showing

33.____

34. You are assisting a mason who is laying up concrete block for an exterior wall. He is careless and there are numerous smears of mortar on the outside surface of blocks which have just been placed. You should

    A.   immediately wipe the mortar off with a wet rag
    B.   allow the mortar to dry before removing it
    C.   use a trowel to scrape it off immediately
    D.   immediately wipe it off with an oily rag

34.____

35. A standard brick weighs, in pounds, about

    A. 1   B. 2   C. 4   D. 8

35.____

Questions 36-40.

DIRECTIONS: Questions 36 through 40, inclusive, refer to the concrete masonry units shown in the sketches below.

36. The unit which is called a stretcher is marked   36.____

    A. 1   B. 2   C. 3   D. 4

37. The unit which would be used to form the sides of door or window openings in a wall is   37.____
marked

    A. 2   B. 4   C. 5   D. 6

38. A 12-inch wall is to be built with a brick facing and concrete block backing. The unit which   38.____
would be required for this wall and would not ordinarily be used in a wall consisting of
concrete block only is marked

    A. 5   B. 6   C. 9   D. 11

39. The unit which would MOST likely be used for an interior non-bearing partition is   39.____

    A. 7   B. 8   C. 10   D. 11

40. The unit which would BEST serve to support a floor joist is marked   40.____

    A. 3   B. 8   C. 9   D. 10

KEY (CORRECT ANSWERS)

1.	C	11.	D	21.	C	31.	B
2.	C	12.	D	22.	B	32.	C
3.	A	13.	C	23.	B	33.	B
4.	A	14.	D	24.	B	34.	B
5.	B	15.	D	25.	A	35.	C
6.	B	16.	A	26.	B	36.	A
7.	D	17.	B	27.	D	37.	C
8.	B	18.	D	28.	B	38.	B
9.	A	19.	D	29.	D	39.	C
10.	D	20.	B	30.	D	40.	B

———

TEST 2

DIRECTIONS: Each question or incomplete statement is followed by several suggested answers or completions. Select the one that BEST answers the question or completes the statement. *PRINT THE LETTER OF THE CORRECT ANSWER IN THE SPACE AT THE RIGHT.*

1. A bricklayer uses a lead in laying brickwork to   1._____

    A. tool joints   B. place mortar beds
    C. cut brick   D. maintain line and grade

2. A masonry unit 9" x 4 1/2" x 2 1/2" weighs two pounds. This unit is MOST probably a(n)   2._____

    A. insulating fire brick
    B. fireclay brick
    C. roman brick
    D. stone-faced concrete block

3. A 1:2:4 concrete contains for each bag of cement   3._____

    A. two wheelbarrows of sand and four of gravel
    B. sand weighing twice as much as a bag of cement and gravel weighing twice as much as the sand
    C. two cubic feet of sand and four of gravel
    D. one bag of lime, two of sand, and four of gravel

4. A short stairway is constructed of brick. The brick forming the nosing of the treads should be   4._____

    A. full headers   B. half headers
    C. stretchers   D. splits

5. On a given job, concrete for a floor is being chuted into place. The lower end of the chute is 8 feet above the floor. The end of the chute can be moved about horizontally. Which one of the following statements is MOST NEARLY correct?   5._____

    A. Moving the end of the chute is poor practice because concrete should be spread from one location.
    B. The 8-foot drop is good practice as it prevents clogging the end of the chute.
    C. The 8-foot drop is poor practice because it causes segregation.
    D. The height of drop is unimportant as long as the end of the chute can be moved about.

6. Terra cotta units would be used in a wall as   6._____

    A. backing
    B. facing
    C. either backing or facing, depending upon type
    D. fireproofing only

7. A carborundum stone would MOST likely be used to   7._____

    A. remove form marks from concrete
    B. form mortar joints in brickwork

C. smooth marble walls
D. dress fieldstone walls

8. If 1,233 bricks are required for 100 square feet of 8-inch wall, the number of bricks required for 150 square feet of 12-inch wall is MOST NEARLY

    A. 2,466   B. 2,569   C. 2,672   D. 2,775

8._____

Questions 9-12.

DIRECTIONS: Questions 9 through 12 refer to the brickwork units shown in the sketches below.

9. Common bond is marked

    A. 1   B. 2   C. 3   D. 4

9._____

10. English bond is marked

    A. 1   B. 2   C. 3   D. 5

10._____

11. The bond marked 6 would be used PRINCIPALLY for

    A. bearing walls   B. veneered walls
    C. faced walls   D. sidewalks

11._____

12. For a wall using face brick with common brick backing and all full headers, the bond which would require the LARGEST number of face brick per 100 square feet is marked

    A. 2   B. 3   C. 4   D. 5

12._____

13. It is CORRECT to say that

    A. bond affects the appearance of the wall only
    B. bond has no effect on the strength of a wall
    C. proper bond increases the strength of a wall
    D. the bond depends only upon the type of brick used to construct the wall

13._____

14. In brick work, *filling in* could not be done on a wall which had a thickness, in inches, of

    A. 8   B. 12   C. 16   D. 20

14._____

15. Projecting courses of masonry at the corners of buildings are known as   15.____

    A. quoins   B. coping   C. culls   D. batters

16. Steel columns in buildings are encased in concrete to   16.____

    A. strengthen the columns
    B. provide a surface for plastering
    C. give protection from fire
    D. comply with architectural plans

17. In concrete work, wooden form spreaders   17.____

    A. are never used
    B. should be removed as soon as the concrete is placed
    C. should be removed after the concrete has attained initial set
    D. should be removed after the concrete has attained final set

18. An advantage of cinder concrete block over stone concrete block is that the cinder con-   18.____
crete block is

    A. stronger   B. heavier
    C. a better insulator   D. better in appearance

19. The use of bats in brickwork is   19.____

    A. good, because it cuts the amount of face brick required
    B. good, because it increases the strength of the wall
    C. sometimes required by the bond
    D. never justified

Questions 20-24.

DIRECTIONS: Questions 20 through 24 refer to the four mortars which are described below.

    Mortar A - 1 part cement, 1/4 part lime putty, 3 parts sand
    Mortar B - 1 part cement, 1 part lime putty, 6 parts sand
    Mortar C - 1 part cement, 2 parts lime putty, 9 parts sand
    Mortar D - 1/4 part cement, 2 parts lime putty, 7 parts sand

20. The mortar to use for reinforced brickwork is Mortar   20.____

    A. A   B. B   C. C   D. D

21. Mortar D would be MOST appropriate for   21.____

    A. masonry work below grade
    B. masonry work in severe (cold) climates
    C. non-bearing walls
    D. furnace linings

22. The mortar that would MOST likely be used for the bearing walls of a two-story building   22.____
is either Mortar

    A. A or B   B. B or C   C. C or D   D. A or D

23. The mortar that would be used to lay insulating fire brick is Mortar 23._____

    A. A   B. B or C
    C. D   D. none of the above

24. Of the following, the kind of bar that would be MOST satisfactory for reinforcing concrete would be one that 24._____

    A. had a rusty surface   B. was covered with grease
    C. was painted   D. was oiled

25. Concrete for a thin, reinforced wall section should have a slump, in inches, of MOST NEARLY 25._____

    A. 1   B. 2 1/2   C. 6   D. 10

26. Within reasonable limits and for a given amount of cement, the MOST important factor governing the strength of concrete is the amount of _____ added. 26._____

    A. water   B. sand and gravel
    C. sand   D. gravel

27. Terrazzo is made of 27._____

    A. clay
    B. marble chips and neat cement
    C. sand and neat cement
    D. asbestos and neat cement

28. The number of cubic feet in 3 cubic yards is 28._____

    A. 81   B. 82   C. 83   D. 84

29. A cubic foot of loose, dry sand would weigh, in pounds, MOST NEARLY 29._____

    A. 25   B. 50   C. 75   D. 100

30. The number of cubic yards in 47 cubic feet is MOST NEARLY 30._____

    A. 1.70   B. 1.74   C. 1.78   D. 1.82

31. A wall 8'0" high by 12'6" long has a window opening 4'0" high by 3'6" wide. The net area of the wall (allowing for the window opening) is, in square feet, 31._____

    A. 86   B. 87   C. 88   D. 89

32. Rafters would be used in the construction of 32._____

    A. roofs   B. floors   C. walls   D. columns

33. A trimmer arch would be used in construction involving 33._____

    A. windows   B. floor openings
    C. chimneys   D. bulkheads

34. Coping would be placed by a 34._____

    A. carpenter   B. mason   C. plumber   D. roofer

35. Before placing concrete in forms, the inside surfaces of the forms should be covered with   35.____

    A. oil   B. water   C. paint   D. wax

36. In laying up ashlar masonry walls, it is good practice to   36.____

    A. pin up the stones with spalls
    B. drop the stones into place
    C. settle each stone in place with a maul
    D. slide stones over stones which have already been laid

37. Of the following materials, the one which is MOST acceptable and commonly used in reinforced concrete construction to form chairs is   37.____

    A. brick   B. wood
    C. wire   D. cinder block

Questions 38-40.

DIRECTIONS: Questions 38 through 40 are to be answered SOLELY in accordance with the information in the paragraph given below.

Before placing the concrete, check that the forms are rigid and well braced, and place the concrete within 45 minutes after mixing it. Fill the forms to the top with the wearing-course concrete. Level off the surfaces with a strikeboard. When the concrete becomes stiff but still workable (in a few hours), finish the surface with a wood float. This fills the hollows and compacts the concrete, and produces a smooth but gritty finish. For a non-gritty and smoother surface (but one that is more slippery when wet), follow up with a steel trowel after the water sheen from the wood-troweling starts to disappear. If you wish, slant the tread forward a fraction of an inch so that it will shed rain water.

38. Slanting the tread a fraction of an inch gives a surface that will   38.____

    A. have added strength   B. not be slippery when wet
    C. shed rain water   D. not have hollows

39. In addition to giving a smooth but gritty finish, the use of a wood float will tend to   39.____

    A. give a finish that is slippery when wet
    B. compact the concrete
    C. give a better wearing course
    D. provide hollows to retain rain water

40. Which one of the following statements is MOST NEARLY correct?   40.____

    A. Having checked the forms, one may place the concrete immediately after mixing same.
    B. One must wait at least 15 minutes after mixing the concrete before it may be placed in the forms.
    C. A gritty compact finish and one which is more slippery when wet will result with the use of a wood float.
    D. A steel trowel used promptly after a wood float will tend to give a non-gritty smooth finish.

KEY (CORRECT ANSWERS)

1. D	11. C	21. C	31. A
2. A	12. A	22. B	32. A
3. C	13. C	23. D	33. C
4. A	14. A	24. A	34. B
5. C	15. A	25. C	35. A
6. C	16. C	26. A	36. C
7. A	17. B	27. B	37. C
8. D	18. C	28. A	38. C
9. A	19. C	29. D	39. B
10. B	20. A	30. B	40. A

EXAMINATION SECTION

TEST 1

DIRECTIONS: Directly and concisely, using brief answer form, answer the following questions.

1. What is meant by "building up a lead?"

2. How often are header courses usually put in common bond brick masonry?

3. What do you set into the wall of a very deep manhole?

4. What kind of joints are used when plaster is to be put directly on the brick?

5. What is meant by "crowding the line?"

6. In what position are bricks laid in the invert of a sewer?

7. What kind of course is used in brick structure to bind the front and back walls together?

8. What is a brick called that has been cut in half lengthwise?

9. What kind of brick is usually cut with a skutch?

10. What is a brick called that is laid flatwise and parallel to the face of the wall?

—

KEY (CORRECT ANSWERS)

1. Building up end section (corner) of wall

2. Every 4 to 8 stretcher courses

3. Manhole steps (rungs) (ladder)

4. Cut off (rough) (vee)

5. Pushing brick too close to gauge line

6. On edge (rowlock)

7. Header course

8. Soap (sop) (queener)

9. Fire brick

10. Stretcher

—

TEST 2

DIRECTIONS: Directly and concisely, using brief answer form, answer the following questions.

1. What is a brick called that is laid on the narrow edge?

2. In coming to a height, if there is a course of brick difference in the level, how would you describe it?

3. What is a course of bricks called that is laid lengthwise?

4. What is used in the middle of a long wall to keep the line level?

5. What are the alternate headers and stretchers laid in the same course called?

6. What is used to tie face brick to the woodwork in brick veneered walls?

7. What is the course called where each course projects one to one and a half inches beyond the course below?

8. What is the usual thickness of manhole brickwork less than 8 feet deep?

9. What is a brick called that is laid at right angles to the face of the wall?

10. What is done to the outside of a manhole?

―

KEY (CORRECT ANSWERS)

1. Rowlock

2. Hog

3. Stretcher course

4. Twig (twigger) (twigging) (tingle)

5. Flemish bond

6. Metal ties

7. Corbel

8. 8 inches

9. Header

10. Plaster with cement mortar (parge)

TEST 3

DIRECTIONS: Directly and concisely, using brief answer form, answer the following questions.

1. Where is radial or round-face brick used?

2. What kind of scaffold is used on the inside of a brick smokestack?

3. What is the operation of filling in the space between a front and back course of brick called?

4. What are bricks called that are laid stretcher fashion, except that every fifth or sixth course is a header course?

5. What is the joint called that slopes into the wall from the top to the bottom of the joint?

6. What are bricks called that are laid in alternate courses of headers and stretchers?

7. What is the course called where the bricks are all set on the end with the narrow sides facing out?

8. What is used to get your courses uniform?

9. What is the course called from which an arch starts?

10. Name four tooled joints.

___

KEY (CORRECT ANSWERS)

1. In arches (round work)

2. Pudlock (putlog)

3. Slushing up (flushing up) (dashing up)

4. Common bond (American) (garden)

5. Struck joint (weather)

6. English bond (Dutch) (diamond)

7. Soldier course (soldiers)

8. Story pole (story rod) (coursing pole) (gauge rod)

9. Skew-back (spring) (springer)

10. Struck
    Raked
    Flush
    Stripped
    Weather
    Vee
    Bead
    Convex
    Concave

BASIC FUNDAMENTALS OF

BRICK AND TILE MASONRY

CONTENTS

BASIC FUNDAMENTALS OF

BRICK AND TILE MASONRY

Section I. CHARACTERISTICS OF BRICK AND BRICK MASONRY

9—1. Terminology

a. Definition. Brick masonry is that type of construction in which units of baked clay or shale of uniform size, small enough to be placed with one hand, are laid in courses with mortar joints to form walls of virtually unlimited length and height. Brick are kiln-baked from various clay and shale mixtures. The chemical and physical characteristics of the ingredients vary considerably; these and the kiln temperatures combine to produce brick in a variety of colors and hardnesses. In some regions, pits are opened and found to yield clay or shale which, when ground and moistened, can be formed and baked into durable brick; in other regions, clays or shales from several pits must be mixed.

b. Brick Sizes. Standard bricks manufactured in the United States are 2¼ by 3¾ by 8 inches. English bricks are 3 by 4½ by 9 inches, Roman bricks are 1½ by 4 by 12 inches, and Norman bricks are 2¾ by 4 by 12 inches. The actual dimensions of brick vary a little because of shrinkage during burning.

c. Cut Brick. Frequently the bricklayer cuts the brick into various shapes. The more common of these are shown in figure 9–1. They are called half or bat, three-quarter closure, quarter closure, king closure, queen closure, and split. They are used to fill in the spaces at corners and such other places where a full brick will not fit.

d. Names of Brick Surfaces. The six surfaces of a brick are called the face, the side, the cull, the end, and the beds, as shown in figure 9–2.

e. Brick Classification. There are three general types of structural clay masonry units: solid masonry units, hollow masonry units and architectural terra cotta. These units may serve a structural function only, as a decorative finish, or a combination of both. Structural clay products include brick, hollow tile of all types and architectural terra cotta. They do not include thin wall tile, sewer pipe, flue linings, drain tile and the like.

HALF OR BAT   THREE-QUARTER CLOSURES   QUARTER CLOSURE

KING CLOSURE   QUEEN CLOSURE   SPLIT

Figure 9–1. Shapes of cut brick.

f. Types of Bricks. There are many types of brick. Some are different in formation and composition while others vary according to their use. Some commonly used types of bricks are:

(1) *Building brick.* The term building brick, formerly called common brick, is applied to brick made of ordinary clays or shales and burned in the usual manner in the kilns. These bricks do not have special scorings or markings and are not produced in any special color or surface texture. Building brick is also known as hard and kiln run brick. It is used generally for the backing courses in solid or cavity brick walls. The harder and more durable kinds are preferred for this purpose.

Figure 9–2. Names of brick surfaces.

(2) *Face brick.* Face brick are used in the exposed face of a wall and are higher quality units than backup brick. They have better durability and appearance. The most common colors of face brick are various shades of brown, red, gray, yellow, and white.

(3) *Clinker brick.* When bricks are over-burned in the kilns, they are called clinker brick. This type of brick is usually hard and durable and may be irregular in shape. Rough hard corresponds to the clinker classification.

(4) *Pressed brick.* The dry press process is used to make this class of brick which has regular smooth faces, sharp edges, and perfectly square corners. Ordinarily all press brick are used as face brick.

(5) *Glazed brick.* This type of brick has one surface of each brick glazed in white or other color. The ceramic glazing consists of mineral ingredients which fuse together in a glass-like coating during burning. This type of brick is particularly suited for walls or partitions in hospitals, dairies, laboratories or other buildings where cleanliness and ease of cleaning is necessary.

(6) *Fire brick.* This type of brick is made of a special type of fire clay which will withstand the high temperatures of fireplaces, boilers and similar usages without cracking or decomposing. Fire brick is generally larger than regular structural brick and often it is hand molded.

(7) *Cored brick.* Cored brick are brick made with two rows of five holes extending through their beds to reduce weight. There is no significant difference between the strength of walls constructed with cored brick and those constructed with solid brick. Resistance to moisture penetration is about the same for both types of walls. The most easily available brick that will meet requirements should be used whether the brick is cored or solid.

(8) *European brick.* The strength and durability of most European clay brick, particularly English and Dutch, compares favorably with the clay brick made in the United States.

(9) *Sand-lime brick.* Sand-lime bricks are made from a lean mixture of slaked lime and fine silicious sand molded under mechanical pressure and hardened under steam pressure. They are used extensively in Germany.

9–2. Strength of Brick Masonry

a. The principal factors governing the strength of brick masonry are:

(1) Strength of the brick.

(2) Strength and elasticity of the mortar.

(3) Workmanship of the bricklayer.

(4) Uniformity of the brick used.

(5) Method used in laying the brick.

b. The strength of an individual brick varies widely, depending upon the material and manufacturing method. Brick with ultimate compressive strengths as low as 1,600 pounds per square inch have been made, whereas some well-burned bricks have compressive strengths exceeding 15,000 pounds per square inch.

c. The strength of portland-cement-lime mortar is normally higher than the strength of the brick. Because of this, the strength of brick masonry laid in cement-lime mortar is higher than the strength of the individual brick. The use of plain lime mortar reduces the load-carrying capacity of a wall or column to considerably less than half the load-carrying capacity of the same type construction in which portland-cement-lime mortar has been used. The compressive working strength of a brick wall or column that has been laid up with cement-lime mortar is normally from 500 to 600 pounds per square inch.

d. High suction brick, if laid dry, will absorb water from the mortar before the bond has developed and, for this reason, such brick must be thoroughly wetted before laying to obtain good masonry construction. In wetting brick, sprinkling is not sufficient. A hose stream should be played on the pile until water runs from all sides, after which the brick should be allowed to surface dry before they are laid. Water on the surface of the brick will cause floating on the mortar bed. A rough but effective on-the-job test for determining whether the brick should be wet before laying is to sprinkle a few drops of water on the flat side of the brick. If these drops of water are absorbed completely in less than 1 minute, the brick should be wet when laid.

9–3. Resistance to Weathering

a. The resistance of masonry walls to weathering depends almost entirely upon their resistance to water penetration because freezing and thawing action is virtually the only type of weathering that affects brick masonry. With the best workmanship, it is possible to build brick walls that will resist the penetration of rain water during a storm lasting as long as 24 hours accompanied by a 50- to 60-mile-per-hour wind. In most construction, it is unreasonable to expect the type of workmanship required to build a wall that will allow no water pentration. It is advisable to provide some means of taking care of moisture after it has penetrated the brick masonry. Properly designed flashing and cavity walls are two ways of handling moisture that has entered the wall.

b. Important factors in preventing the entrance of water are tooled mortar joints and caulking around windows and door frames.

c. The joints between the brick must be solidly filled, especially in the face tier. Slushing or grouting the joints after the brick has been laid does not completely fill the joint. The mortar joint should be tooled to a concave surface before the mortar has had a chance to set up. In tooling, sufficient force should be used to press the mortar tight against the brick on both sides of the mortar joint.

d. Mortar joints that are tightly bonded to the brick have been shown to have greater resistance to moisture penetration than joints not tightly bonded to the brick.

9–4. Fire Resistance

Fire-resistance tests conducted upon brick walls laid up with portland-cement-lime mortar have made it possible to give fire-resistance periods for various thicknesses of brick walls. A summary is given in table 9–1. The tests were made using the American Society for Testing Materials standard method for conducting fire tests.

9–5. General characteristics of Brick Masonry

a. *Heat-Insulating Properties.* Solid brick masonry walls provide very little insulation against heat and cold. A cavity wall or a brick wall backed with hollow clay tile has much better insulating value.

b. *Sound-Insulating Properties.* Because brick walls are exceptionally massive, they have good sound-insulating properties. In general, the heavier the wall, the better will be its sound-insulating value; however, there is no appreciable increase in sound insulation by a wall more than 12 inches thick as compared to a wall between 10 and 12 inches thick. The expense involved in constructing a thicker wall merely to take advantage of the slight increase is too great to be worthwhile. Dividing the wall into two or more layers, as in the case of a cavity wall, will increase its resistance to the transmission of sound from one side of the wall to the other. Brick walls are poor absorbers of sound originating within the walls and reflect much of it back into the structure. Sounds caused by impact, as when the wall is struck with a hammer, will travel a great distance along the wall.

c. *Expansion and Construction.* Brick masonry expands and contracts with temperature change. Walls up to a length of 200 feet do not need expansion joints. Longer walls need an expansion joint for every 200 feet of wall. The joint can be made as shown in figure 4–26. A considerable amount of the expansion and contraction is taken up in the wall itself. For this reason, the amount of movement that theoretically takes place does not actually occur.

d. *Abrasion Resistance.* The resistance of brick to abrasion depends largely upon its compressive strength, related to the degree of burning. Well-burned brick have excellent wearing quantities.

e. *Weight of Brick.* The weight of brick varies from 100 to 150 pounds per cubic foot depending upon the nature of the materials used in making the brick and the degree of burning. Well-burned brick are heavier than under-burned brick.

Table 9–1. Fire Resistance of Brick Load-Bearing Walls Laid with Portland Cement Mortar

Normal wall thickness (inches)	Type of wall	Material	Ultimate fire-resistance period. Incombustible members framed into wall or not framed in members		
			No plaster (hours)	Plaster on one side* (hours)	Plaster on two sides* (hours)
4	Solid	Clay or shale	1¼	1¾	2½
8	Solid	Clay or shale	5	6	7
12	Solid	Clay or shale	10	10	12
8	Hollow rowlock	Clay or shale	2½	3	4
12	Hollow rowlock	Clay or shale	5	6	7
9 to 10	Cavity	Clay or shale	5	6	7
4	Solid	Sand-lime	1¾	2½	3
8	Solid	Sand-lime	7	8	9
12	Solid	Sand-lime	10	10	12

*Not less than ½ inch of 1:3 sanded gypsum plaster is required to develop these ratings.

Section II. BRICKLAYING METHODS

9-6. Fundamentals

Good bricklaying procedure depends on good workmanship and efficiency. Means of obtaining good workmanship are treated below. Efficiency involves doing the work with the fewest possible motions. The bricklayer studies his own operations to determine those motions that are unnecessary. Each motion should have a purpose and should accomplish a definite result. After learning the fundamentals, every bricklayer develops his own methods for achieving maximum efficiency. The work must be arranged in such a way that the bricklayer is continually supplied with brick and mortar. The scaffolding required must be planned before the work begins. It must be built in such a way as to cause the least interference with other workmen. Masons' tools and equipment which are generally the same or similar to those used in bricklaying are discussed in paragraphs 7-1 and 7-2.

9-7. Types of Bonds

The word bond, when used in reference to masonry, may have three different meanings:

a. Structural Bond. Structural bond is the method by which individual masonry units are interlocked or tied together to cause the entire assembly to act as a single structural unit. Structural bonding of brick and tile walls may be accomplished in three ways. First, by overlapping (interlocking) the masonry units, second by the use of metal ties imbedded in connecting joints, and third by the adhesion of grout to adjacent wythes of masonry.

b. Mortar Bond. Mortar bond is the adhesion of the joint mortar to the masonry units or to the reinforcing steel.

c. Pattern Bond. Pattern bond is the pattern formed by the masonry units and the mortar joints on the face of a wall. The pattern may result from the type of structural bond used or may be purely a decorative one in no way related to the structural bond. There are five basic pattern bonds in common use today (fig. 9-3): running bond, common or American bond, Flemish bond, English bond, and block or stack bond.

(1) *Running bond.* This is the simplest of the

Figure 9-3. Some types of brick masonry bond.

basic pattern bonds, the running bond consists of all stretchers. Since there are no headers used in this bond, metal ties are usually used. Running bond is used largely in cavity wall construction and veneered walls of brick, and often in facing tile walls where the bonding may be accomplished by extra width stretcher tile.

(2) *Common or American bond.* Common bond is a variation of running bond with a course of full length headers at regular intervals. These headers provide structural bonding as well as pattern. Header courses usually appear at every fifth, sixth, or seventh course depending on the structural bonding requirements. In laying out any bond pattern it is very important that the corners be started correctly. For common bond, a "three-quarter" brick must start each header course at the corner. Common bond may be varied by using a Flemish header course.

(3) *Flemish bond.* Each course of brick is made up of alternate stretchers and headers, with the headers in alternate courses centered over the stretchers in the intervening courses. Where the headers are not used for the structural bonding, they may be obtained by using half brick, called "blind-headers." There are two methods used in starting the corners. Figure 9–3 shows the so

called "Dutch" corner in which a three-quarter brick is used to start each course and the "English" corner in which 2 inch or quarter-brick closures must be used.

(4) *English bond.* English bond is composed of alternate courses of headers and stretchers. The headers are centered on the stretchers and joints between stretchers in all courses line up vertically. Blind headers are used in courses which are not structural bonding courses.

(5) *Block or stack bond.* Stack bond is purely a pattern bond. There is no overlapping of the units, all vertical joints being alined. Usually this pattern is bonded to the backing with rigid steel ties, but when 8 inch thick stretcher units are available, they may be used. In large wall areas and in load-bearing construction, it is advisable to reinforce the wall with steel pencil rods placed in the horizontal mortar joints. The vertical alinement requires dimensionally accurate units, or carefully prematched units, for each vertical joint alinement. Variety in pattern may be achieved by numerous combinations and modifications of the basic patterns shown.

(6) *English cross or Dutch bond.* This bond is a variation of English bond and differs only in that vertical joints between the stretchers in alter-

Figure 9–4. Masonry units and mortar joints.

nate courses do not line up vertically. These joints center on the stretchers themselves in the courses above and below.

d. Masonry Terms. Specific terms are used to describe the various positions of masonry units and mortar joints in a wall (fig. 9–4):

(1) *Course.* One of the continuous horizontal layers (or rows) of masonry which, bonded together, form the masonry structure.

(2) *Wythe.* A continuous vertical 4-inch or greater section or thickness of masonry as the thickness of masonry separating flues in a chimney.

(3) *Stretcher.* A masonry unit laid flat with its longest dimension parallel to the face of the wall.

(4) *Header.* A masonry unit laid flat with its longest dimension perpendicular to the face of the wall. It is generally used to tie two wythes of masonry together.

(5) *Rowlock.* A brick laid on its edge (face).

(6) *Bull-Stretcher.* A rowlock brick laid with its longest dimension parallel to the face of the wall.

(7) *Bull-Header.* A rowlock brick laid with its longest dimension perpendicular to the face of the wall.

(8) *Soldier.* A brick laid on its end so that its longest dimension is parallel to the vertical axis of the face of the wall.

e. Metal Ties. Metal ties can be used to tie the brick on the outside face of the wall to the backing courses. These are used when no header courses are installed. They are not as satisfactory as header courses. Typical metal ties are shown in figure 9–5.

f. Flashing. Flashing is installed in masonry construction to divert moisture, which may enter the masonry at vulnerable spots, to the outside. Flashing should be provided under horizontal masonry surfaces such as sills and copings, at intersections of masonry walls with horizontal surfaces such as roof and parapet or roof and chimney, over heads of openings such as doors and windows, and frequently at floor lines, depending upon the type of construction. To be most effective, the flashing should extend through the outer face of the wall and be turned down to form a drop. Weep holes should be provided at intervals of 18 inches to 2 feet to permit the water which accumulates on the flashing to drain to the outside. If, because of appearance, it is necessary to stop the flashing back of the face of the wall, weep holes are even more important than when the flashing extends through the wall. Concealed flashing with tooled mortar joints frequently will retain water in the wall for long periods and, by concentrating moisture at one spot, may do more harm than good.

9–8. Mortar Joints and Pointing

a. Holding the Trowel. The trowel should be held firmly in the position shown in figure 9–6. The thumb should rest on top of the handle and should not encircle it.

b. Picking up Mortar. A right-handed bricklayer picks up mortar with the left edge of the trowel from the outside of the pile (1, fig. 9–7). He picks up the correct amount of spread for one

Figure 9–5. Metal ties.

Figure 9–6. Correct way to hold a trowel.

to five bricks, according to the wall space and his skill. A pickup for one brick forms a small windrow along the left edge of the trowel. A pickup for five bricks is a full load for a large trowel (2, fig. 9–7).

c. Spreading Mortar. Holding the trowel with its left edge directly over the centerline of the previous course, the bricklayer tilts the trowel slightly and moves it to the right, dropping a windrow of mortar along the wall unit until the trowel is empty (3, fig. 9–7). In some instances mortar will be left on the trowel when the spreading of mortar on the course below has been completed. When this occurs the remaining mortar is returned to the board. A right-handed bricklayer works from left to right along the wall.

d. Cutting Off Mortar. Mortar projecting beyond the wall line is cut off with the trowel edge (step 1, fig 9–8) and thrown back on the mortar board, but enough is retained to "butter" the left

end of the first brick to be laid in the fresh mortar.

e. Bed Joint. With the mortar spread about 1 inch thick for the bed joint as shown in step 1, figure 9–8, a shallow furrow is made (step 2, figure 9–8) and the brick pushed into the mortar (step 3, figure 9–8). If the furrow is too deep, there will be a gap left between the mortar and the brick bedded in the mortar. This gap will reduce the resistance of the wall to water penetration. The mortar for a bed joint should not be spread out too far in advance of the laying. A distance of 4 or 5 bricks is advisable. Mortar that has been spread out too far will dry out before the brick is bedded in it. This results in a poor bond as can be seen by figure 9–9. The mortar must be soft and plastic so that the brick can be easily bedded in it.

f. Head Joint. The next step after the bed joint mortar has been spread is the laying of the brick. The brick to be laid is picked up as shown in figure

1 Proper way to pick up mortar

3 Mortar thrown on brick

2 Trowel full of mortar

4 Mortar spread for a distance of 3 to 5 brick

Figure 9–7. Picking up and spreading mortar.

Step 1

Step 2

Step 3

Figure 9–8. Bed joint and furrow.

Figure 9–9. A poorly bonded brick.

9–10 with the thumb on one side of the brick and the fingers on the other. As much mortar as will stick is placed on the end of the brick. The brick should then be pushed into place so that excess mortar squeezes out at the head joint and at the sides of the wall as indicated in figure 9–11. The head joint must be completely filled with mortar. This can only be done by placing plenty of mortar on the end of the brick. After the brick is bedded, the excess mortar is cut off and used for the next end joint. Surplus mortar should be thrown to the back of the mortar board for retempering if necessary. The proper position of the brick is determined by the use of a cord which can be seen in step 1, figure 9–14.

Figure 9–10. Proper way to hold a brick.

Figure 9–11. Head joint in a stretcher course.

g. Method of Inserting Brick in Wall. The method of inserting a brick in a space left in a wall is shown in figure 9–12. A thick bed of mortar is spread (step 1, fig. 9–12) and the brick shoved into this deep bed of mortar (step 2, fig. 9–12) until squeezes out at the top of the joint at the face tier, and at the header joint (step 3, fig. 9–12) so that the joints are full of mortar at every point.

h. Cross Joints in Header Courses. The position of a cross joint is illustrated in figure 9–13. These joints must be completely filled with mortar. The mortar for the bed joint should be spread several brick widths in advance. The mortar is spread over the entire side of the header brick before it is placed in the wall (step 1, fig. 9–13). The brick is then shoved into place so that the mortar is forced out at the top of the joint and the excess mortar cut off, as shown in step 2, figure 9–13.

i. Closure Joints in Header Courses. Figure 9–14 shows the method of laying a closure brick in a header course. Before laying the closure brick, plenty of mortar should be placed on the sides of the brick already in place (step 1, fig. 9–14). Mortar should also be spread on both sides of the closure brick to a thickness of about 1 inch (step 2, fig. 9–14). The closure brick should then be laid in position without disturbing the brick already in place (step 3, fig. 9–14).

j. Closure Joints in Stretcher Courses. Before laying a closure brick for a stretcher course, the ends of the brick on each side of the opening to be filled with the closure brick should be well covered with mortar (step 1, fig. 9–15). Plenty of mortar should then be thrown on both ends of the closure brick (step 2, fig. 9–15) and the brick laid without

disturbing those already in place (step 3, fig. 9–15). If any of the adjacent brick are disturbed they must be removed and relaid. Otherwise,

Step 1

Step 2

Step 3

Figure 9–12. Laying inside brick.

Step 1

Step 2

Figure 9–13. Making cross joints in header courses.

cracks will form between the brick and mortar, allowing moisture into the wall.

k. Thickness of Mortar Joints. There is no hard and fast rule regarding the thickness of the mortar joint. Brick that are irregular in shape may require mortar joints up to ½-inch thick. All brick irregularities are taken up in the mortar joint. Mortar joints ¼ inch thick are the strongest and should be used when the bricks are regular enough to permit it.

l. Slushed Joints. Slushed joints are those made by depositing the mortar on the head joints in order that the mortar will run down between the brick to form a solid joint. *This should not be done.* Even when the space between the brick is completely filled, there is no way to compact the mortar against the faces of the brick and *a poor bond will result.*

m. Pointing. Filling exposed joints with mortar immediately after the wall has been laid is called pointing. Pointing is frequently necessary to fill

Step 1

Step 2

Step 3

Figure 9–14. Making closure joints in header courses.

Step 1

Step 2

Step 8

Figure 9–15. Making closure joints in stretcher courses.

holes and correct defective mortar joints. The pointing trowel is used for this purpose.

9–9. Cutting Brick

a. Cutting with Bolster or Brick Set. If a brick is to be cut to exact line the bolster or brick set should be used. When using these tools, the straight side of the cutting edge should face the part of the brick to be saved and also face the bricklayer. One blow of the hammer on the brick set should be enough to break the brick. Extremely hard brick will need to be cut roughly with the head of the hammer in such a way that there is enough brick left to be cut accurately with the brick set. See figure 9–16.

b. Cutting with the Hammer. For normal cutting work, such as is required for making the closures and bats required around openings in walls and for the completion of corners, the brick hammer should be used. The first step is to cut a line all the way around the brick with light blows of the hammer head (fig. 9–17). When the line is complete, a sharp blow to one side of the cutting line will split the brick at the cutting line. Rough places are trimmed using the blade of the hammer, as shown in figure 9–17. The brick can be held in the hand while being cut.

9–10. Joint Finishes

a. Exterior Surfaces. Exterior surfaces of mortar joints are finished to make the brickwork more waterproof and to improve the appearance. There are several types of joint finishes, as shown in figure 9–18. The more important of these are discussed below. When joints are cut flush with the brick and not finished, cracks are immediately apparent between the brick and the mortar. Although these cracks are not deep, they are undesirable and can be eliminated by finishing or tooling the joint. In every case, the mortar joint should be finished before the mortar has hardened to any appreciable extent. The jointing tool is shown in figure 7–1.

b. Concave Joint. The best joint from the standpoint of weather-tightness is the concave joint. This joint is made with a special tool after the excess mortar has been removed with the trowel. The tool should be slightly larger than the joint. Force is used to press the mortar tight against the brick on both sides of the mortar joint.

c. Flush Joint. The flush joint (fig. 9–18) is made by keeping the trowel almost parallel to the face of the wall while drawing the point of the trowel along the joint.

d. Weather Joint. A weather joint sheds water more easily from the surface of the wall and is formed by pushing downward on the mortar with the top edge of the trowel.

1 Striking brick to one side of cutting line

Figure 9-16. Cutting brick with a bolster.

2 Trimming rough spots

Figure 9-17. Cutting brick with a hammer.

WALL SURFACE

JOINT

BRICK

CONCAVE   FLUSH   STRUCK   WEATHER   RAKED   BEAD

Figure 9-18. Joint finishes.

Section III. BRICK CONSTRUCTION

9-11. Bricktender's Duties

a. The bricktender mixes mortar, carries brick and mortar to the bricklayer, and keeps him supplied with these materials at all times. He fills the mortar board and places it in a position convenient for the bricklayer. He assists in the layout and, at times, such as during rapid backup bricklaying, he may lay out brick in a line on an adjacent course so that the bricklayer needs to move each brick only a few inches in laying backup work.

b. Wetting brick is also the duty of the bricktender. This is done when bricks are laid in warm weather. There are four reasons for wetting brick just before they are laid:

(1) There will be a better bond between the brick and the mortar.

(2) The water will wash dust and dirt from the surface of the brick. Mortar adheres better to a clean brick.

(3) If the surface of the brick is wet, the mortar spreads more evenly under it.

(4) A dry brick may absorb water from the mortar rapidly. This is particularly bad when mortar containing portland cement is used. In order for cement to harden properly, sufficient moisture must be present to complete the hydration of the cement. If the brick robs the mortar of too much water, there will not be enough left to hydrate the cement properly.

9-12. Bricklayer's Duties

The bricklayer does the actual laying of the brick. It is his responsibility to lay out the job so that the finished masonry will be properly done. In construction involving walls, he must see that the walls are plumb and the courses level.

FOURTH COURSE

THIRD COURSE

FOOTING AND FOUNDATION COMPLETED

FIRST AND SECOND COURSE

Figure 9-19. Wall footing.

9-13. Footings

a. Wall Footing.

(1) A footing is required under a wall when the bearing capacity of the supporting soil is not sufficient to withstand the wall load without a further means of redistribution. The footing must be wider than the thicknes of the wall, as illustrated in figure 9-19. The required footing width and thickness for walls of considerable height or for walls that are to carry a heavy load should be determined by a qualified engineer. Every footing should be below the frost line in order to prevent heaving and settlement of the foundation. For the usual one-story building with an 8-inch-thick wall, a footing 16 inches wide and approximately 8 inches thick as given in figure 9-19 is usually enough. Although brickwork footings are satisfactory, footings are normally concrete, leveled on top to receive the brick or stone foundation wall.

(2) As soon as the subgrade is prepared, the bricklayer should place a bed of mortar about 1 inch thick on the subgrade to take up all irregularities. The first course of the foundation is laid on this bed of mortar. The other courses are then laid on this first course (fig. 9-19).

b. Column Footing. A column footing for a 12- by 16-inch brick column is shown in figure 9-20. The construction method for this footing is the same as for the wall footing.

9-14. Eight-Inch Common Bond Brick Wall

a. Laying Out the Wall. For a wall of given

Figure 9-20. Column footing.

Figure 9-21. Determination of vertical brick joints and number of brick in one course.

length, the bricklayer makes a slight adjustment in the width of head joints so that some number of brick, or some number including one half-brick, will just make up the length. The bricklayer first lays the brick on the foundation without mortar (fig. 9-21). The distance between the bricks is equal to the thickness of the head mortar joints. Tables 9-2, 9-3, and 9-4 give the number of courses and horizontal joints required for a given wall height.

b. Laying Corner Leads. The corners are erected first. This is called "laying of leads." The bricklayer will use these leads as a guide in laying the remainder of the wall. Step 3, figure 9-23 shows a corner lead laid up and racked so that the center portion of the wall can be bonded into the corner lead. Only the face tier is laid in these corners and the corner lead is built up above the rest of the wall a distance of six or seven courses or to the height of the next header course above. Normally the first course is a header course.

(1) The first step in laying a corner lead is shown in first step, figure 9-22. Two three-quarter closures are cut and a 1-inch thick mortar bed is laid on the foundation. The three-quarter closure marked by *a* in second step, figure 9-22 is pressed down into the mortar bed until the bed joint becomes ½ inch thick. Next, mortar is placed on the end of three-quarter closure *b* and a head joint is formed as described in paragraph 9-8. The head joint between the two three-quarter closures should be ½ inch thick also. Excess mortar that has been squeezed out of the joints is cut off. The level of the two three-quarter closures should now be checked by means of the plumb rule placed in the positions indicated by the heavy dashed lines in second step, figure 9-22. The edges of both these closure bricks must be even with the outside face of the foundation.

(2) Next mortar is spread on the side of brick *c* and it is laid as shown in third step, figure 9-22. Its level is checked using the plumb rule in the

Table 9-2. Height of Courses: 2¼-Inch Brick, ⅜-Inch Joint

Courses	Height	Courses	Height	Courses	Height	Courses	Height	Courses	Height
1	0' 2⅝"	21	4' 7⅛"	41	8' 11⅝"	61	13' 4⅛"	81	17' 8⅝"
2	0' 5¼"	22	4' 9¾"	42	9' 2¼"	62	13' 6¾"	82	17' 11¼"
3	0' 7⅞"	23	5' 0⅜"	43	9' 4⅞"	63	13' 9⅜"	83	18' 1⅞"
4	0' 10½"	24	5' 3"	44	9' 7½"	64	14' 0"	84	18' 4½"
5	1' 1⅛"	25	5' 5⅝"	45	9' 10⅛"	65	14' 2⅝"	85	18' 7⅛"
6	1' 3¾"	26	5' 8¼"	46	10' 0¾"	66	14' 5¼"	86	18' 9¾"
7	1' 6⅜"	27	5' 10⅞"	47	10' 3⅜"	67	14' 7⅞"	87	19' 0⅜"
8	1' 9"	28	6' 1½"	48	10' 6"	68	14' 10½"	88	19' 3"
9	1' 11⅝"	29	6' 4⅛"	49	10' 8⅝"	69	15' 1⅛"	89	19' 5⅝"
10	2' 2¼"	30	6' 6¾"	50	10' 11¼"	70	15' 3¾"	90	19' 8¼"
11	2' 4⅞"	31	6' 9⅜"	51	11' 1⅞"	71	15' 6⅜"	91	19' 10⅞"
12	2' 7½"	32	7' 0"	52	11' 4½"	72	15' 9"	92	20' 1½"
13	2' 10⅛"	33	7' 2⅝"	53	11' 7⅛"	73	15' 11⅝"	93	20' 4⅛"
14	3' 0¾"	34	7' 5¼"	54	11' 9¾"	74	16' 2¼"	94	20' 6¾"
15	3' 3⅜"	35	7' 7⅞"	55	12' 0⅜"	75	16' 4⅞"	95	20' 9⅜"
16	3' 6"	36	7' 10½"	56	12' 3"	76	16' 7½"	96	21' 0"
17	3' 8⅝"	37	8' 1⅛"	57	12' 5⅝"	77	16' 10⅛"	97	21' 2⅝"
18	3' 11¼"	38	8' 3¾"	58	12' 8¼"	78	17' 0¾"	98	21' 5¼"
19	4' 1⅞"	39	8' 6⅜"	59	12' 10⅞"	79	17' 3⅜"	99	21' 7⅞"
20	4' 4½"	40	8' 9"	60	13' 1½"	80	17' 6"	100	21' 10½"

position given in third step, figure 9–22. Its end must also be even with the outside face of the foundation. Brick *d* is laid and its level and position checked. When brick *d* is in the proper position, the quarter closures *e* and *f* should be cut and placed according to the recommended procedure described for laying closure brick. All excess mortar should be removed and the tops of these quarter closures checked to see that they are at the same level as the tops of surrounding brick.

(3) Brick *g* (fourth step, fig. 9–22) is now shoved into position after mortar has been spread on its face. Excess mortar should be removed. Bricks *h*, *i*, *j*, and *k* are laid in the same manner. The level of the brick is checked by placing the plumb rule in the several positions indicated in fourth step, figure 9–22. All brick ends must be flush with the surface of the foundation. Bricks *l*, *m*, *n*, *o*, and *p* are then laid in the same manner. The number of leader bricks that must be laid in the first course of the corner lead can be determined from fifth step, figure 9–22. It will be noted that six header bricks are required on each side of the three-quarter closures a and b.

Table 9-3. Height of Courses: 2¼-Inch Brick, ½-Inch Joint

Courses	Height	Courses	Height	Courses	Height	Courses	Height	Courses	Height
1	0' 2¾"	21	4' 9¾"	41	9' 4¾"	61	13' 11¾"	81	18' 6¾"
2	0' 5½"	22	5' 0½"	42	9' 7½"	62	14' 2½"	82	18' 9½"
3	0' 8¼"	23	5' 3¼"	43	9' 10¼"	63	14' 5¼"	83	19' 0¼"
4	0' 11"	24	5' 6"	44	10' 1"	64	14' 8"	84	19' 3"
5	1' 1¾"	25	5' 8¾"	45	10' 3¾"	65	14' 10¾"	85	19' 5¾"
6	1' 4½"	26	5' 11½"	46	10' 6½"	66	15' 1½"	86	19' 8½"
7	1' 7¼"	27	6' 2¼"	47	10' 9¼"	67	15' 4¼"	87	19' 11¼"
8	1' 10"	28	6' 5"	48	11' 0"	68	15' 7"	88	20' 2"
9	2' 0¾"	29	6' 7¾"	49	11' 2¾"	69	15' 9¾"	89	20' 4¾"
10	2' 3½"	30	6' 10½"	50	11' 5½"	70	16' 0½"	90	20' 7½"
11	2' 6¼"	31	7' 1¼"	51	11' 8¼"	71	16' 3¼"	91	20' 10¼"
12	2' 9"	32	7' 4"	52	11' 11"	72	16' 6"	92	21' 1"
13	2' 11¾"	33	7' 6¾"	53	12' 1¾"	73	16' 8¾"	93	21' 3¾"
14	3' 2½"	34	7' 9½"	54	12' 4½"	74	16' 11½"	94	21' 6½"
15	3' 5¼"	35	8' 0¼"	55	12' 7¼"	75	17' 2¼"	95	21' 9¼"
16	3' 8"	36	8' 3"	56	12' 10"	76	17' 5"	96	22' 0"
17	3' 10¾"	37	8' 5¾"	57	13' 0¾"	77	17' 7¾"	97	22' 2¾"
18	4' 1½"	38	8' 8½"	58	13' 3½"	78	17' 10½"	98	22' 5½"
19	4' 4¼"	39	8' 11¼"	59	13' 6¼"	79	18' 1¼"	99	22' 8¼"
20	4' 7"	40	9' 2"	60	13' 9"	80	18' 4"	100	22' 11"

Table 9–4. Height of Courses: 2¼-Inch Brick, ⅝-Inch Joint

Courses	Height	Courses	Height	Courses	Height	Courses	Height	Courses	Height
1	0' 2⅞"	21	5' 0⅜"	41	9' 9⅞"	61	14' 7⅜"	81	19' 4⅞"
2	0' 5¾"	22	5' 3¼"	42	10' 0¾"	62	14' 10¼"	82	19' 7¾"
3	0' 8⅝"	23	5' 6⅛"	43	10' 3⅝"	63	15' 1⅛"	83	19' 10⅝"
4	0' 11½"	24	5' 9"	44	10' 6½"	64	15' 4"	84	20' 1½"
5	1' 2⅜"	25	5' 11⅞"	45	10' 9⅜"	65	15' 6⅞"	85	20' 4⅜"
6	1' 5¼"	26	6' 2¾"	46	11' 0¼"	66	15' 9¾"	86	20' 7¼"
7	1' 8⅛"	27	6' 5⅝"	47	11' 3⅛"	67	16' 0⅝"	87	20' 10⅛"
8	1' 11"	28	6' 8½"	48	11' 6"	68	16' 3½"	88	21' 1"
9	2' 1⅞"	29	6' 11⅜"	49	11' 8⅞"	69	16' 6⅜"	89	21' 3⅞"
10	2' 4¾"	30	7' 2¼"	50	11' 11¾"	70	16' 9¼"	90	21' 6¾"
11	2' 7⅝"	31	7' 5⅛"	51	12' 2⅝"	71	17' 0⅛"	91	21' 9⅝"
12	2' 10½"	32	7' 8"	52	12' 5½"	72	17' 3"	92	22' 0½"
13	3' 1⅜"	33	7' 10⅞"	53	12' 8⅜"	73	17' 5⅞"	93	22' 3⅜"
14	3' 4¼"	34	8' 1¾"	54	12' 11¼"	74	17' 8¾"	94	22' 6¼"
15	3' 7⅛"	35	8' 4⅝"	55	13' 2⅛"	75	17' 11⅝"	95	22' 9⅛"
16	3' 10"	36	8' 7½"	56	13' 5"	76	18' 2½"	96	23' 0"
17	4' 0⅞"	37	8' 10⅜"	57	13' 7⅞"	77	18' 5⅜	97	23' 2⅞"
18	4' 3¾"	38	9' 1¼"	58	13' 10¾"	78	18' 8¼"	98	23' 5¾"
19	4' 6⅝"	39	9' 4⅛"	59	14' 1⅝"	79	18' 11⅛"	99	23' 8⅝"
20	4' 9½"	40	9' 7"	60	14' 4½"	80	19' 2"	100	23' 11½"

(4) The second course, a stretcher course, is now laid. Procedure is shown in step 1, figure 9–23. A 1-inch thick layer of mortar should be spread over the first course and a shallow furrow made in the mortar bed. Brick *a* (step 2, figure 9–23) is then laid in the mortar bed and shoved down until the mortar joint is ½-inch thick. Brick *b* may now be shoved into place after mortar has been spread on its end. Excess mortar is removed and the joint checked for thickness. Bricks *c*, *d*, *e*, *f*, and *g* are laid in the same manner and checked to make them level and plumb. The level is checked by placing the plumb rule in the position indicated in step 2, figure 9–23. The bricks are plumbed by using the plumb rule in a vertical position as shown in figure 9–24. This should be done in several places. As may be determined from 3, figure 9–23, seven bricks are required for the second course. The remaining bricks in the corner lead are laid in the manner described for the bricks in the second course.

(5) Since the portion of the wall between the leads is laid using the leads as a guide, the level of the courses in the lead must be checked continually, and after the first few courses the lead is plumbed. If the brickwork is not plumb, bricks must be moved in or out until the lead is accurately plumb. It is not good practice to move brick much once they are laid in mortar; therefore, care is taken to place the brick accurately at the start. Before the mortar has set, the joints are tooled or finished.

(6) A corner lead at the opposite end of the wall is built in the same manner. It is essential that the level of the tops of corresponding courses be the same in each lead; that is, the top of the second course in one corner lead must be at the same height above the foundation as the second course in the other corner lead. A long 2-by 2-inch pole can be used to mark off the heights of the different courses above the foundation. This pole can be used to check the course height in the corner leads. The laying of leads is closely supervised and only skilled men are employed in this work.

c. Laying the Face Tier Between the Corner Leads.

(1) With the corner leads at each end of the wall completed, the face tier of brick for the wall between the leads is laid. It is necessary to use a line, as shown in figure 9–25. Nails are driven into the top of the mortar joint as shown in figure 9–25. The line is hung over the nails and pulled taut by means of weights attached to each end. The line is positioned 1/16 inch outside the wall face level with the top of the brick.

(2) With the line in place, the first or header course is laid in place between the two corner leads, as described in paragraph 9–8. The brick is shoved into position so that its top edge is 1/16 inch behind the line. Do not crowd the line. If the corner leads are accurately built, the entire wall will be level and plumb. It is not necessary to use

FIRST STEP IN LAYING CORNER

SECOND STEP

THIRD STEP

FOURTH STEP

FIFTH STEP

Figure 9–22. First course of corner lead for 8-inch common bond brick wall.

the level on the section of the wall between the leads; however, it is advisable to check it with the level at several points. For the next course, the line is moved to the top of the next mortar joint. The brick in the stretcher course should be laid as described in paragraph 9–8. Finish the face joints before the mortar hardens.

d. Laying the Back Tier.

(1) When the face tier of brick for the wall between the leads has been laid up to but not including the second header course, normally six courses, the backup tier is laid. Procedure for laying backup brick has already been described. The backup brick for the corner leads are laid first and the remaining brick afterwards (fig. 9–26). The line need not be used for the backup brick in an 8-inch wall. When the backup brick have been laid up to the height of the second header course, the second header course is laid.

FOUNDATION

MORTAR

FIRST COURSE (HEADERS)

Step 1

FIRST COURSE (HEADERS)

SECOND COURSE FACE TIER (STRETCHERS)

FOUNDATION

CAREFULLY REMOVE EXCESS MORTAR

g

f

c

a   b   d   e

Step 2

THREE QUARTER CLOSURES

THREE QUARTER CLOSURES

3 Completed corner lead

Figure 9-23. Second course of corner lead for 8-inch common bond brick wall.

Figure 9-24. Plumbing a corner.

(2) The wall for the entire building is built up to a height including the second header course at which time corner leads are continued six more courses. The wall between the leads is constructed as before and the entire procedure repeated until the wall has been completed to the required height.

9-15. Twelve-Inch Common Bond Brick Wall

The 12-inch-thick common bond brick wall is laid out as shown in 3, figure 9-27. Note that the construction is similar to that for the 8-inch wall with the exception that a third tier of brick is used. The header course is laid (1, fig. 9-27) first and the corner leads built. Two tiers of backing brick are required instead of one. The second course is shown in 2, figure 9-27 and the third course in 3, figure 9-27. Two header courses are required and they overlap as shown in 1, figure 9-27. A line should be used for the inside tier of backing brick for a 12-inch wall.

9-16. Protection of Brickwork and Use of a Trig

a. Protection the Brick. The tops of all brick walls should be protected each night from rain damage by placing boards or tarpaulins on top of the wall and setting loose bricks on them.

b. Use of a Trig. When a line is stretched on a long wall, a trig is used to prevent sagging and to keep it from being blown in or out from the face of the wall by the wind. The trig consists of a

Figure 9–25. Use of the line.

short piece of line looped around the main line and fastened to the top edge of a brick that has been previously laid in proper position. A lead between the corner leads must be erected in order to place the trig brick in its proper location.

9–17. Window and Door Openings

a. Window Openings.

(1) If windows are to be installed in the wall, openings are left for them as the bricklaying proceeds. The height to the top of one full course should be exactly the height of the window sill. When the distance from the foundation to the bottom of the window sill is known, the bricklayer can determine how many courses are required to bring the wall up to that height. If the sill is to be

Figure 9–26. Backing brick at the corner—8-inch common bond brick wall.

THREE-QUARTER CLOSURES

STRETCHERS

QUARTER CLOSURES

HEADERS EVERY SIXTH OR SEVENTH COURSE

THREE-QUARTER CLOSURES

1 First course of 12-inch common bond wall

QUARTER CLOSURES

2 Second course of 12-inch common bond wall

Figure 9–27. Twelve-inch common bond wall.

4 feet 4¼ inches above the foundation and ½-inch mortar joints are to be used, 19 courses will be required. (Each brick plus one mortar joint is 2¼ + ½ = 2¾ inches. One course is thus 2¾ inches high. Four feet 4¼ inches divided by 2¾ is 19, the number of courses required.)

(2) With the brick laid up to sill height, the rowlock sill course is laid as shown in figure 9–28. The rowlock course is pitched downward. The slope is away from the window and the rowlock course normally takes up a vertical space equal to two courses of brick. The exterior surface of the

3   Third course of 12-inch common bond wall

Figure 9-27.—Continued.

joints between the brick in the rowlock course must be carefully finish to make them watertight.

(3) The window frame is placed on the rowlock sill as soon as the mortar has set. The window frame must be temporarily braced until the brickwork has been laid up to about one-third the height of the window frame. These braces are not removed for several days in order that the wall above the window frame will set properly. Now the bricklayer lays up the brick in the rest of the wall in such a way that the top of the brick in the course at the level of the top of the window frame is not more than 1/4 inch above the frame. To do this, he marks on the window frame with a pencil the top of each course. If the top course does not come to the proper level, he changes the thickness of the joints slightly until the top course is at the proper level. The corner leads should be laid up af-

ter the height of each course at the window is determined.

(4) The mortar joint thickness for the corner leads is made the same as that determined at the window opening. With the corner leads erected, the line is installed as already described and is stretched across the window opening. The brick can now be laid in the rest of the wall. If the window openings have been planned properly, the brick in the face tier can be laid with a minimum of brick cutting.

b. Placing Lintel Over Window Opening. Lintels are placed above windows and doors to carry the weight of the wall above them. They rest on the brick course that is level or approximately level with the frame head, and are firmly bedded in mortar at the sides. Any space between the window frame and the lintel is closed with blocking and weatherstripped with bituminous materials. The wall is then continued above the window after the lintel is placed.

c. Door Openings. The same procedure can be used for laying brick around a door opening as was used for laying brick around a window opening, including placement of the lintel. The arrangement at a door opening is given in figure 9–29. Pieces of wood cut to the size of a half closure are laid in mortar as brick to provide for anchoring the door frame by means of screws or nails. These wood blocks are placed at several points along the top and sides of the door opening to allow for plumbing the frame.

9–18. Lintels

a. The brickwork above openings in walls must be supported by lintels. Lintels can be made of

FRAME

SILL

HEADER COURSE

ROWLOCK COURSE TILTED

Figure 9-28.   Construction of a window opening.

Figure 9–29. Construction at a door opening.

steel, precast reinforced concrete beams, or wood. The use of wood should be avoided as much as possible. If reinforced brick masonry is employed, the brick above the wall opening can be supported by the proper installation of steel reinforcing bars. This is discussed in paragraph 9–34. Figures 9–30 and 9–31 illustrate some of the methods of placing lintels for different wall thicknesses. The

relative placement and position is determined both by wall thickness and the type of window being used.

b. Usually the size and type of lintels required are given on drawings for the structure. When not given, the size of double-angle lintels required for various width openings in an 8-inch and 12-inch wall can be selected from table 9–5. Wood lintels for various width openings are also given in table 9–5.

c. Installation of a lintel for an 8-inch wall is shown in figure 9–30. The thickness of the angle for a two-angle lintel should be ¼ inch. This makes it possible for the two-angle legs that pro-

1. STEEL LINTEL

2. PRECAST REINFORCED CONCRETE LINTEL

Figure 9–30. Lintels for an 8-inch wall.

Figure 9–31. Lintels for a 12-inch wall.

Table 9–5. Lintel Sizes

Wall thickness	Span					
	3 feet		4 feet* steel angles	5 feet* steel angles	6 feet* steel angles	
	Steel angles	Wood				
8″	2–3 x 3 x ¼	2 x 8 2–2 x 4	2–3 x 3 x ¼	2–3 x 3 x ¼	2–3½ x 3½ x ¼	
12″	2–3 x 3 x ¼	2 x 12 2–2 x 6	2–3 x 3 x ¼	2–3½ x 3½ x ¼	2–3½ x 3½ x ¼	

	7 feet* steel angles	8 feet* steel angles
	2–3½ x 3½ x ¼	2–3½ x 3½ x ¼
	2–4 x 4 x ¼	2–4 x 4 x 4¼

*Wood lintels should not be used for spans over 3 feet since they burn out in case of fire and allow the brick to fall.

ject up into the brick to fit exactly in the ½-inch joint between the face and backing-up ties of an 8-inch wall.

9–19. Corbeling

a. Corbeling consists of courses of brick set out beyond the face of the wall in order to form a self-supporting projection. This type of construction is shown in figure 9–32. The portion of a chimney that is exposed to the weather is frequently corbeled out and increased in thickness to improve its weathering resistance. Headers should also be used as much as possible in corbeling. It is usually necessary to use various-sized bats. The first projecting course may be a stretcher course if necessary. No course should extend out more than 2 inches beyond the course below it and the total projection of the corbeling should not be more than the thickness of the wall.

b. Corbeling must be done carefully for the construction to have maximum strength. All mortar joints should be carefully made and completely filled with mortar. When the corbeled-out brick masonry is to withstand large loads, a qualified engineer should be consulted.

9–20. Brick Arches

a. *Characteristics.* If properly constructed, a brick arch can support a heavy load. The ability to support loads is derived primarily from its curved shape. Several arch shapes can be used; the circular and elliptical shapes are most common (fig. 9–33). The width of the mortar joint is less at the bottom of the brick than it is at the top, and it should not be thinner than ¼ inch at any point. Arches made of brick must be constructed with full mortar joints. As laying progresses, care must be taken to see that the arch does not bulge out of position.

b. *Use of Temporary Support.*

(1) A brick arch is constructed on a temporary support that is left in position until the mortar has set. The temporary support is made of wood as shown in figure 9–34. The dimensions required are obtained from drawings. For arches up to 6 feet in span, ¾-inch plywood should be used for temporary supports. Two pieces cut to the proper curved shape are made and nailed to 2 by 4's placed between them. This will provide a wide-enough surface to support the brick adequately.

CORBELING

Figure 9–32. Corbeled brick wall.

ELLIPTICAL ARCH

CIRCULAR ARCH

Figure 9-33. Types of arches.

(2) The temporary support should be held in position with wedges that can be driven out when the mortar has hardened enough for the arch to be self-supporting.

c. Laying the Arch. Construction of an arch is begun at the two ends or abutments of the arch. The brick is laid from each end toward the center or crown. The key or middle brick is the last to be placed. There should be an odd number of brick in order for the key or middle brick to come at the exact center of the arch. The arch should be laid out in such a way that no brick need be cut.

d. Determination of the Brick Spacing. The best way to determine the number of brick required for an arch is to lay a temporary support on its side on level ground and set brick around it. Adjust the spacing until the key brick comes at the exact center of the arch. When this has been done, the position of the brick can be marked on the temporary support to be used as a guide when the arch is actually built.

9-21. Watertight Walls

a. General.

(1) The water that passes through brick walls does not usually enter through the mortar or brick but through cracks between brick and mortar. Sometimes these cracks are formed because the bond between the brick and mortar is poor. They are more apt to occur in head joints than in bed joints. To prevent this, some brick must be wetted. If the position of the brick is changed after the mortar has begun to set, the bond between the brick and mortar will be destroyed and a crack will result. Shrinkage of the mortar is also frequently responsible for the formation of cracks.

(2) Both the size and number of cracks between the mortar and the brick can be reduced if the exterior face of all the mortar joints is tooled to a concave finish. All head joints and bed joints must be completely filled with mortar if watertightness is to be obtained.

b. Parging. A procedure found effective in producing a leakproof wall is shown in figure 9-35. The back of the brick in the face tier is plastered with not less than 3/8 inch of rich cement mortar before the backing bricks are laid. This is called parging or back plastering. Since parging should not be done over mortar protruding from the joints, all joints on the back of the face tier of bricks must be cut flush.

c. Membrane Waterproofing. Membrane waterproofing should be used if the wall is subject to considerable water pressure. The membrane, if

Figure 9-34. Use of a templet in arch construction.

Figure 9-35. Parging.

properly installed, is able to adjust to any shrinkage or settlement without cracking. If the wall is to be subjected to considerable ground water or the surrounding soil is impervious, tile drains, or French drains if drainage tile is not available, should be constructed around the base of the wall (fig. 9–36).

d. Waterproof Coatings.

(1) *Bituminous mastic.* For a foundation wall below ground level, two coats of bituminous mastic applied to the outside surface of the brick will yield satisfactory results. Asphalt or coal-tar pitch may be used and applied with mops.

(2) *Waterproof paints.* The watertightness of brick walls above ground level is improved by the application of transparent waterproof paints such as a water solution of sodium silicate. Varnish is also effective. When used, these paints should be applied as specified by the manufacturer. Certain white and colored waterproofing paints are also available. In addition, good results have been obtained by the use of high-quality oil base paints.

(3) *Portland-cement paint.* Portland-cement paint generally gives excellent results. The brick wall should be at least 30 days old before the portland-cement paint is applied and all efflorescence must be removed from the surface to be painted (para. 9–27). Type 2, class A portland-cement paint should be used (Fed. Spec. TT-P-21 (2)). Manufacturer's instructions for mixing and applying the paint are to be followed. Surfaces must be

damp when the paint is applied. A water spray is the best means of wetting the surface. Whitewash or calcimine type brushes are used to apply the paint. Portland-cement paint can be applied with a spray gun but its rain resistance will be reduced.

e. Repairing Cracks. Before transparent waterproof paints or portland-cement paint is applied, all cracks should be repaired.

(1) *Cracks in mortar joints.* Cracks in mortar joints are repaired by chipping out the mortar in the joint the full width of the joint to a depth of about 2 inches. The hole formed is carefully cleaned out by scrubbing with clean water. While the surface is still wet, a coating of cement mortar, made with sufficient water to form a thick liquid, should be applied. Before this coating sets, the hole should be filled with the prehydrated mortar described in paragraph 9–26 which is recommended for use in tuckpointing.

(2) *Cracks in brick.* Cracks in the brick should be repaired the same as cracks in concrete (para 5–35, 5–36).

9–22. Fire-Resistant Brick

a. Purpose. Fire brick are manufactured for such uses as lining furnaces and incinerators. Their purpose is to protect the supporting structure or outer shell from intense heat. This outer shell may consist of common brick or, in some cases, steel, neither of which has good heat resistance.

b. Types of Fire-Resistant Brick. There are two types of fire-resistant brick:

(1) *Fire brick.* These bricks are made from a special clay known as fire clay. They will withstand high temperatures and are heavier and usually larger than common brick. The standard size is 9 by 4½ by 2½ inches.

(2) *Silica brick.* Silica brick should be used if resistance to acid gases is required. Silica brick should not be used if it is to be alternately heated and cooled. Most incinerators, therefore, should be lined with fire brick rather than silica brick.

c. Laying Fire Brick. Thin joints are of the utmost importance in laying fire brick. This is especially true when the brick are exposed to high temperatures such as those occurring in incinerators. The brick should be kept in a dry place until the time they are used.

(1) *Mortar.* The mortar to be used in laying fire brick consists of fire clay mixed with water. The consistency of the mortar should be that of

LOOSE STONE

4" TILE DRAIN

WHEN TILE DRAIN IS OMITTED, THE DRAIN IS CALLED A FRENCH DRAIN

Figure 9–36. Drain around foundation.

thick cream. Fire clay can be obtained by grinding used fire brick.

(2) *Laying procedure.* The brick is dipped in the mortar in such a way that all faces except the top face are covered. The brick is then tapped firmly in place with a bricklayer's hammer. The joint between the brick should be as thin as possible and the brick should fit tightly together. Any cracks between the fire brick will allow heat to penetrate to the outside shell of the incinerator or furnace and damage it. The fire brick in one course lap those in the course below by one-half brick. The heat joints are thus staggered in the same way as they are staggered in the usual type of brick construction.

d. Laying Silica Brick. Silica brick are laid without mortar. They fit so closely that they fuse together at the joints when subjected to high temperatures. The head joints for silica brick are staggered, as for fire brick.

9-23. Special Types of Walls

a. Solid Walls. Many different types of walls may be built of brick. The solid 8- and 12-inch walls in common bond are the ones usually used for solid wall construction in the United States. The most important of the hollow walls are the cavity wall and the rowlock type wall.

b. Cavity Walls.

(1) Cavity walls provide a means of obtaining a watertight wall that may be plastered without the use of furring or lathing. From the outside they appear the same as solid walls without header courses (fig. 9–37). No headers are required because the two tiers of brick are held together by means of metal ties installed every sixth course and on 24-inch centers. To prevent waterflow to the inside tier, ties must be angled in a downward direction from the inside tier to the outside tier.

(2) The 2-inch cavity between the two tiers of brick provides a space down which water that penetrates the outside tier may flow without passing through to the inside of the wall. The bottom of the cavity is above ground level and is drained by weep holes placed in the vertical joints between two bricks in the first course of the outer tier. These holes may be formed by leaving the mortar out of some of the vertical joints in the first course. The holes should be spaced at about 24-inch intervals. The air space also gives the wall better heat and sound insulation properties.

Figure 9–37. Details for a cavity wall.

c. Rowlock-Back Wall.

(1) One type of rowlock wall is shown in figure 9–38. The face tier of this wall has the same appearance as a common bond wall with a full header course every seventh course. The backing tier is laid with the brick on edge. The face tier and backing tier are tied together by a header course as shown. A 2-inch space is provided between the two tiers of brick, as for a cavity wall.

(2) An all-rowlock wall is constructed with brick in the face and backing tier both laid on edge. The header course would be installed at every fourth course: three rowlock courses to every header course.

(3) A rowlock wall is not as watertight as the cavity wall. Water is able to follow any crack present in the header course and pass through the wall to the inside surface.

d. Partition Walls. Partition walls that carry very little load can be made using one tier of brick only. This produces a wall 4 inches thick. A wall of this thickness is laid up without headers.

e. Laying Brick for Special Type Walls. Brick are laid in cavity walls and partition walls according to the procedure given in paragraph 9–8 for making bed joints, head joints, cross joints, and closures. The line is used the same as for a common bond wall. Corner leads for these walls

HEADERS

INTERIOR

2" AIR SPACE

EXTERIOR

Figure 9–38. Details of a rowlock backwall.

are erected first and the wall between is built up afterward.

9–24. Manholes

a. Purpose.

(1) Manholes are required for sewers so they can be cleaned and inspected. The size of the manhole required depends largely upon the size of the sewer. Manholes should be circular or oval, since this reduces the stress arising from both water and soil pressure. For small sewers on a straight line, a 4-foot diameter manhole is satisfactory. Details of a typical manhole are given in figure 9–39.

(2) Both bottom and walls may be made of brick but normally the bottom is made of concrete because it is easier to cast the required shape in concrete rather than form it of brick. The walls of the manhole can be economically constructed if brick is used, eliminating the need for form work.

b. Required Wall Thickness. The thickness of walls required depends on the depth and the diame-

ter of the manhole. An 8-inch thick wall should be used for manholes up to 8 feet in diameter and less than 15 feet deep. Manholes over 15 feet should be designed by a qualified engineer.

c. Manhole Construction.

(1) Only headers are used for an 8-inch wall. A line cannot be used in the construction of the manhole wall. The level is employed to make sure that all brick in a course are at the same level. The straightedge or a straight, surfaced 2 by 4 may be used to span the manhole and the plumb rule placed on the 2 by 4 to determine whether the brick rises at the same level all around the manhole. Since the manhole wall will not be seen, some irregularities in brick position and mortar joint thickness are permissible. All joints in this type of wall are bed joints, or closure joints, made as described in paragraph 9–8.

(2) Before the first course of brick is laid, a bed of mortar 1-inch thick should be placed on the foundation and the first course laid on this mortar bed.

(3) To reduce the size of the manhole to that required for the manhole frame and cover, the brick is corbeled inward as shown (2, fig. 9–39). One brick should not project more than 2 inches beyond the brick below it. Upon completion of the manhole wall, it is plastered on the outside with the same mortar used in laying the brick. The thickness of the mortar coating should be at least $\frac{3}{8}$ inch.

(4) The base of the manhole frame is placed in a 1-inch thick mortar bed spread on top of the manhole wall. The wrought-iron steps shown should be spaced at about 15 inches vertically and the embedded part placed in a cross mortar joint.

9–25. Method of Supporting Beams

a. When it is necessary to support a wood beam on a brick wall, it may be done as shown in 1, figure 9–40. Note the wall tie. If possible, the mortar should be kept away from the beam for dry rot may result if the wood is completely encased in mortar. This may be conveniently done by means of the wall box shown in 2, figure 9–40. The end of the beam should be cut at an angle which, in case of fire, will permit it to fall without damaging the wall above the beam. The beam should bear on the full width of the inside tier of brick for either an 8-inch or 12-inch wall.

b. If a steel beam is to be supported on a brick wall, a steel bearing plate set in mortar should be used under the beam. This bearing plate, when

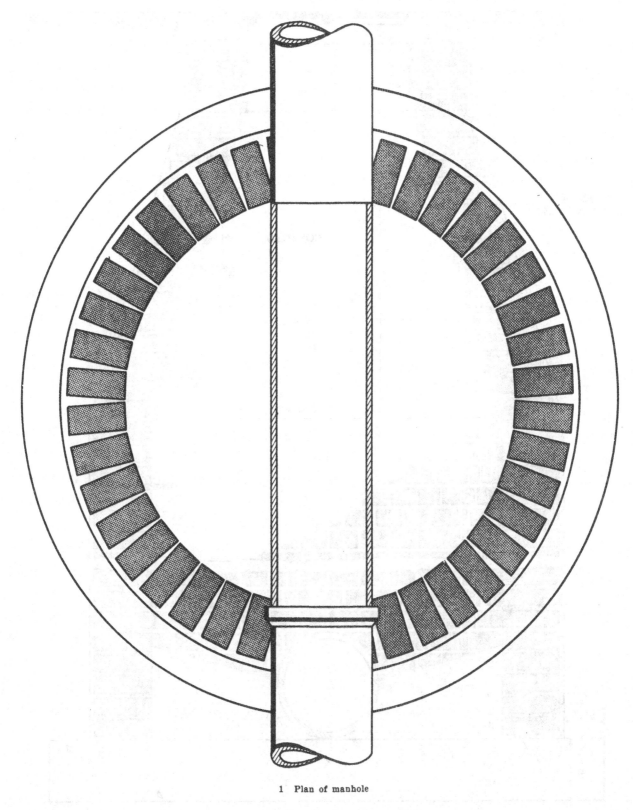

1 Plan of manhole

Figure 9–39. Details of a sewer manhole.

properly designed, reduces the tendency for the steel beam to crush the brick. The size of the bearing plate depends upon the size of beam and the load the beam carries. The method for determining the required thickness of bearing plates is beyond the scope of this manual.

2   Brick manhole cross section

Figure 9-39.—Continued.

1 Wall tie

2 Beam box

*Figure 9–40. Details of a wood beam supported
by a brick wall.*

9–26. Maintenance and Repair of Brick Walls

If a brick masonry wall is properly constructed, it requires little maintenance or repair. The proper repair of old masonry can be more expensive than the complete removal and replacement of the disintegrated portion. The use of good mortar, proper finishing of joints, and adequate flashing adds little to the initial cost and reduces the cost of maintenance throughout the life of the masonry.

a. Tuck-Pointing. Tuck-pointing consists of cut-ting out all loose and disintegrated mortar to a depth of at least ½ inch and replacing it with new. If leakage is to be stopped, all the mortar in the affected area should be cut out and new mortar placed according to instructions given in paragraph 9–21e. Tuck-pointing done as routine maintenance requires the removal of the defective mortar only.

b. Preparation of the Mortar Joint. All dust and loose material should be removed by brush or by means of a water jet after the cutting has been completed. A chisel with a cutting edge about ½-inch wide is suitable for cutting. If water is used in cleaning the joints, no further wetting is required. If not, the surface of the joint must be moistened.

c. Mortar for Tuck-Pointing. The mortar to be used for tuck-pointing should be portland-cement-lime, prehydrated type S mortar, or prehydrated prepared mortar made from type II masonary cement (para 7–3). The prehydration of mortar greatly reduces the amount of shrinkage. The procedure for prehydrating mortar is as follows: The dry ingredients for the mortar are mixed with just enough water to produce a damp mass of such consistency that it will retain its form when compressed into a ball with the hands. The mortar should then be allowed to stand for at least 1 hour and not more than 2 hours. After this has been done, it is mixed with the amount of water required to produce a stiff but workable consistency.

d. Filling the Joint. Sufficient time should be allowed for absorption of the moisture used in preparing the joint before the joint is filled with mortar. Filling the joint with mortar is called re-pointing and is done with a pointing trowel. The prehydrated mortar that has been prepared as above is packed tightly into the joint in thin layers about ¼ inch thick and finished to a smooth concave surface with a pointing tool. The mortar is pushed into the joint with a forward motion in one direction from a starting point to reduce the possibility of forming air pockets.

9–27. Cleaning New Brick Masonry and Removing Efflorescence

a. Cleaning New Brick Masonry. A skilled bricklayer is able to construct a masonry wall that is almost free of mortar stains. Most new brick walls, however, will need some cleaning.

(1) Upon completion of the work, the large particles of mortar adhering to the brick are re-

moved with a putty knife or chisel. Mortar stains are removed with acid prepared by mixing one part commercial muriatic acid with nine parts water. Pour the acid into the water. Before applying the acid, soak the surface thoroughly with water to prevent the mortar stain from being drawn into the pores of the brick.

(2) The acid solution is applied with a long-handled, stiff-fiber brush. Proper precautions must be taken to prevent the acid from getting on hands, arms, and clothing. Goggles are worn to protect the eyes. An area of 15 to 20 square feet is scrubbed with acid and then immediately washed down with clear water. All acid must be removed before it can attack the mortar joint. Door and window frames must be protected from the acid.

b. Removing Efflorescence. Efflorescence is a white deposit of soluble salts frequently appearing on the surface of brick walls. These soluble salts are contained in the brick. Water penetrating the wall dissolves out the salts and when the water evaporates the salt remains. Efflorescence cannot occur unless both water and the salts are present. The proper selection of brick and a dry wall will keep efflorescence to a minimum. It may be removed, however, with the acid solution recommended for cleaning new walls. Acid should be used only after it has been determined that scrubbing with water and stiff brushes will not remove the efflorescence.

9–28. Cleaning Old Brick Masonry

a. Methods. Sand blasting, steam with water jets, and the use of cleaning compounds are the principal methods of cleaning old brick masonry. The process used depends upon the materials used in the wall and the nature of the stain. Many cleaning compounds that have no effect upon brick will damage mortar. Rough-textured brick is more difficult to clean than smooth-textured brick. Often it cannot be cleaned without removing part of the brick itself, and changing the appearance of the wall.

b. Sand Blasting. This method consists of blowing hard sand through a nozzle against the surface to be cleaned. Compressed air forces the sand through the nozzle. A layer of the surface is removed to the depth required to remove the stain. This is a disadvantage in that the surface is given a rough texture upon which soot and dust collect. Sand blasting usually cuts deeply into the mortar joints and it is often necessary to repoint them. After the sand blasting has been completed, it is advisable to apply a transparent waterproofing paint to the surface to help prevent soiling of the wall by soot and dust. Sand blasting is never done on glazed surfaces. A canvas screen placed around the scaffold used for sand blasting will make it possible to salvage most of the sand.

c. Steam With Water Jets.

(1) Cleaning by this method is accomplished by projecting a finely divided spray of steam and water at a high velocity against the surface to be cleaned. Grime is removed effectively without changing the texture of the surface, which gives it an advantage over sand blasting.

(2) The steam may be obtained from a portable truck-mounted boiler. The pressure should be from 140 to 150 pounds per square inch and about 12 boiler horse-power per cleaning nozzle is required. The velocity with which the steam and water spray hits the wall is more important than the volume of spray used.

(3) A garden hose may be used to carry the water to the cleaning nozzle. Another garden hose supplies rinsing water. The operator experiments with the cleaning nozzle in order to determine the best angle and distance from the wall to hold the nozzle. The steam and water valves may also be regulated until the most effective spray is obtained. No more than a 3-foot-square area should be cleaned at one time. The cleaning should be done by passing the nozzle back and forth over the area, then rinsing it immediately with clean water before moving to the next space.

(4) Sodium carbonate, sodium bicarbonate, or trisodium phosphate may be added to the cleaning water entering the nozzle to aid the cleaning action. The amount of salt remaining can be reduced considerably by washing the surface down with water before and after cleaning.

(5) Hardened deposits that cannot be removed by steam cleaning should be removed with steel scrapers or wire brushes. Care must be taken not to cut into the surface. After the deposit has been removed, the surface should be washed down with water and steam cleaned.

d. Cleaning Compounds. There are a number of cleaning compounds that may be used, depending upon the stain to be removed. Most cleaning compounds contain material that will appear as efflorescence if allowed to penetrate the surface. This may be prevented if the surface to be cleaned is thoroughly wetted first. Whitewash, calcimine, and coldwater paints may be removed by the use of a solution of one part hydrochloric acid to five parts water. Fiber brushes are used to scrub the surface vigorously with the solution while the solution is still foaming. When the coating has been removed, the wall must be washed down with clean water until the acid is completely removed.

e. Paint Removers. Oil paint, enamels, varnishes, shellacs, and glue sizings should be removed with a paint remover applied with a brush and left on until the coating is soft enough to be scraped off with a putty knife. The following are effective paint removers:

(1) Commercial paint removers. If these are used, follow the manufacturer's instructions.

(2) Two pounds of trisodium phosphate in 1 gallon of hot water.

(3) One and one-half pounds of caustic soda in 1 gallon of hot water.

(4) Sand blasting or burning with a blowtorch.

f. Removal of Miscellaneous Stains.

(1) *Iron stains.* The cleaning solution is prepared by mixing seven parts of lime-free glycerine with a solution of one part sodium citrate in six parts lukewarm water. Whiting or kieselguhr is added to make a thick paste to be applied to the stain with a trowel and scraped off when dry. The procedure is repeated until the stain in removed. After this the surface must be washed down with water.

(2) *Tobacco stains.* The cleaning solution is prepared by dissolving 2 pounds of trisodium phosphate in 5 quarts of water. In an enameled pan, mix 12 ounces of chloride of lime in enough water to make a smooth thick paste. The trisodium phosphate solution is then mixed with the paste in a 2-gallon stoneware jar. When the lime has settled, the clear liquid is drawn off and diluted with an equal amount of water. A stiff paste is made by mixing the clear liquid with powdered talc; it is applied to the stain with a trowel and the surface washed.

(3) *Smoke stains.* A smooth stiff paste made from trichlorethylene and powdered talc is effective in removing smoke stains. The solution container should be covered to prevent evaporation. If after several applications a slight stain still remains, the surface should be washed down and the procedure recommended for the removal of tobacco stains used. This solution should not be used in an unventilated space for the fumes are harmful.

(4) *Copper and bronze stains.* These stains can be removed with a solution made by mixing one part of ammonium chloride (sal ammoniac) in dry form with four parts of powdered talc. Ammonia water is added and the solution stirred until a thick paste is obtained. This is applied to the stain with a trowel and allowed to dry. Several applications may be necessary after which the surface must be washed down with clear water.

(5) *Oil stains.* Oil stains are effectively removed with a solution consisting of one part trisodium phosphate and 1 gallon of water to which enough whiting has been added to form a paste. The paste should be troweled over the stain in a layer ½ inch thick and allowed to dry for 24 hours. The paste is removed and the surface washed with clean water.

9–29. Flashing

a. Description.

(1) Flashing is the impervious membrane placed at certain places in brick masonry for the purpose of excluding water or to collect any moisture that does penetrate the masonry and directing it to the outside of the wall. Flashing is installed at the head and sill of window openings and, in some buildings, at the intersection of the wall and roof. Where chimneys pass through the roof, the flashing should extend entirely through the chimney wall and turn up for a distance of 1 inch against the flue lining.

(2) The edges of the flashing are turned up as shown in figure 9–41 to prevent drainage into the wall. Flashing is always installed in mortar joints. Drainage for the wall above the flashing is provided by placing ¼-inch cotton-rope drainage wicks in the mortar joint just above flashing membrane at 18 inch spacings. Drainage may also be provided by holes left after dowels placed in the proper mortar joint are removed.

b. Flashing Materials. Copper, lead, aluminum, and bituminous roofing paper may be used for the flashing membrane. Copper is generally preferred but it will stain the masonry when it weathers. If this staining is undesirable, lead-coated copper should be used. Bituminous roofing papers are the cheapest but they are not as durable and may have to be replaced for permanent construction. The cost of replacement is many times the cost of installing high-quality flashing. Corrugated copper flashing sheets are available that produce a good bond with the mortar. These sheets have interlocking watertight joints at points of overlap.

c. Installation of Flashing.

(1) In placing flashing, a ½-inch thick bed of mortar is spread on top of the brick and the flash-

FLASHING

PLASTER WALL

STEEL
LINTEL

WINDOW HEAD

GLASS PANE

1   Window head

Figure 9–41.   Flashing at window opening.

GLASS PANE

WINDOW JAMB

PLASTER WALL

FLASHING

2 Window joint

Figure 9–41.—Continued.

ing sheet pushed firmly down into the mortar. The brick or sill that goes on top of the flashing is forced into a ½-inch thick mortar bed spread on the flashing.

(2) Details for the proper installation of flashing at the head and at the sill of a window are shown in figure 9–41. Note that at the steel lintel the flashing goes in under the face tier of brick, then back of the face tier, and finally over the top of the lintel.

(3) The flashing required at the intersection of the roof and wall is shown in figure 9–42 and is always installed to prevent leakage between the roof and the wall. The upper end of the flashing is fitted and caulked into the groove of the raggle block.

9–30. Protection Against Freezing During Constructoin

a. Precaution. Leaky masonry walls can be attributed to the freezing of mortar before it set or to the lack of protection of materials and walls during cold weather construction. During cold weather, all materials and walls should be protected against freezing temperatures by:

(1) Proper storage of materials.

(2) Proper preparation of mortar.

(3) Heating of masonry units.

(4) Laying precautions.

(5) Protection of work.

b. Storing of Materials. Carelessness in storing materials during cold weather construction encourages poor workmanship, since the removal of ice and snow and the thawing of masonry units are absolutely necessary before construction proceeds. All masonry units and mortar materials should be thoroughly covered with tarpaulins or building paper and stored on plank platforms thick enough or raised high enough to prevent absorption of moisture from the ground.

c. Preparation of Mortar. Water and sand should be heated not to exceed 160° F. and the temperature of the mortar when used should be at least 70° F. and not more than 120° F. On small jobs where mortar boxes are used, they should be of steel and raised about a foot above the ground so that provisions can be made to supply some sort of heat to keep the mortar warm after mixing. *Salt should never be added to mortar to lower its freezing point.*

d. Heating of Masonry Units. To prevent sud-

FLASHING

RAGGLE BLOCK

CAULK

4″ FELT STRIPS

BASE FLASHING

Figure 9–42. Flashing at intersection of roof and wall.

den cooling of the warm mortar in contact with cold units it is recommended that all masonry units be heated to a unit temperature of about 40° F. when the outside temperature is below 18° F. The heating of masonry units requires careful planning. Where required, inside storage should be provided so that heat may be supplied at minimum expense.

e. Laying Precautions. In below freezing weather, brick having high rates of absorption should be sprinkled with *warm* water *just* before laying. Masonry units should never be laid on snow- or ice-covered beds because there will be little or no bond between the mortar and masonry units when the base thaws. Tops of unfinished walls should be kept carefully covered when work is not proceeding. If the covering is displaced and ice or snow collects on the wall top, it should be removed with live steam before the work continues.

f. Protection of Work. Protection of the masonry from freezing is necessary and will vary with weather conditions. Each job is an individual problem. Job layout, desired rate of construction, and the prevailing weather conditions will determine the amount of protection and the type of heat necessary to maintain temperatures within the wall above freezing unit the mortar has set properly.

g. Temperature Variation. When the outside air temperature is below 40 °F., the temperature of the masonry when laid should be above 40° F. An air temperature of above 40° F. should be maintained on both sides of the masonry for at least 48 hours, if type M or S mortar is used, and for at least 72 hours if type N mortar is used. These periods may be reduced to 24 and 48 hours respectively, if high-early-strength cement is used. It is significant to note that the use of high-early-strength cement in mortars does not appreciably alter their rate of set. However, it does increase their rate of gaining strength, thereby providing greater resistance to further injury from freezing.

9-31. Quantities of Material Required for Brick Masonry

See table 9-6 for the quantity of brick and mortar required for various wall thicknesses.

Table 9-6. Quantities of Material Required for Brick Walls*

| Wall area sq ft | Wall thickness in inches | | | | | | | |
| | 4 inches | | 8 inches | | 12 inches | | 16 inches | |
	Number of bricks	Cu ft mortar	Number of bricks	Cu ft mortar	Number of bricks	Cu ft mortar	Number of bricks	Cu ft mortar
1	6.17	.08	12.33	.2	18.49	.32	24.65	.44
10	61.7	.8	123.3	2	184.9	3.2	246.5	4.4
100	617	8	1,233	20	1,849	32	2,465	44
200	1,234	16	2,466	40	3,698	64	4,930	88
300	1,851	24	3,699	60	5,547	96	7,395	132
400	2,468	32	4,932	80	7,396	128	9,860	176
500	3,085	40	6,165	100	9,245	160	12,325	220
600	3,712	48	7,398	120	11,094	192	14,790	264
700	4,319	56	8,631	140	12,943	224	17,253	308
800	4,936	64	9,864	160	14,792	256	19,720	352
900	5,553	72	10,970	180	16,641	288	22,185	396
1,000	6,170	80	12,330	200	18,490	320	24,650	440

*Quantities are based on ½-inch-thick mortar joint. For ⅜-inch-thick joint use 80 percent of these quantities. For ⅝-inch-thick joint use 120 percent.

BASIC FUNDAMENTALS OF

BRICK AND TILE MASONRY

CONTENTS